OCS Report
MMS 2009-064

Outer Continental Shelf
Estimated Oil and Gas Reserves
Gulf of Mexico
December 31, 2006

U.S. Department of the Interior
Minerals Management Service
Gulf of Mexico OCS Region

OCS Report
MMS 2009-064

Outer Continental Shelf

Estimated Oil and Gas Reserves
Gulf of Mexico
December 31, 2006

Authors

T. Gerald Crawford
Grant L. Burgess
Steven M. Haley
Peter F. Harrison
Clark J. Kinler
Gregory D. Klocek
Nancy K. Shepard

Resource Evaluation Office
Reserves Section

Published by

U.S. Department of the Interior
Minerals Management Service
Gulf of Mexico OCS Regional Office

New Orleans
December 2009

Contents

Abstract

As of December 31, 2006, proved reserves in the Gulf of Mexico Outer Continental Shelf (OCS) are estimated to be 20.30 billion barrels of oil and 183.7 trillion cubic feet of gas from 1,229 proved fields. Proved reserves are the total of the cumulative production plus remaining proved reserves. This number includes 34 proved fields that were added during 2006. It also includes the 273 proved fields that have produced and expired. It does not include the 59 unproved active fields. Estimates are derived for individual reservoirs from geologic mapping and reserve evaluation. Cumulative production from the proved fields accounts for 15.08 billion barrels of oil and 166.8 trillion cubic feet of gas. Remaining proved reserves are estimated to be 5.22 billion barrels of oil and 16.9 trillion cubic feet of gas. These reserves are recoverable from 956 proved active fields.

Unproved reserves are estimated to be 4.44 billion barrels of oil and 8.3 trillion cubic feet of gas. These reserves are associated with the 59 unproved active fields studied and the unproved reserves in proved fields. In total, there are 1,015 proved and unproved active fields located in Federal waters. The unproved reserves, associated with the proved and unproved active fields studied, are not added to proved reserves because of different levels of economic certainty and hydrocarbon assurance. For any field spanning State and Federal waters, reserves are estimated for the Federal portion only.

In addition to the proved and unproved reserves discussed above, there are 1.32 billion barrels of oil and 7.7 trillion cubic feet of gas that are not presented in the tables and figures of this report. This oil and gas occurs on leases that have not yet qualified (and therefore have not been placed in a field) or they occur as known resources in proved fields, or as known resources in unproved fields. As further drilling and development occur, additional hydrocarbon volumes will become reportable, and MMS anticipates future proved and unproved reserves to increase.

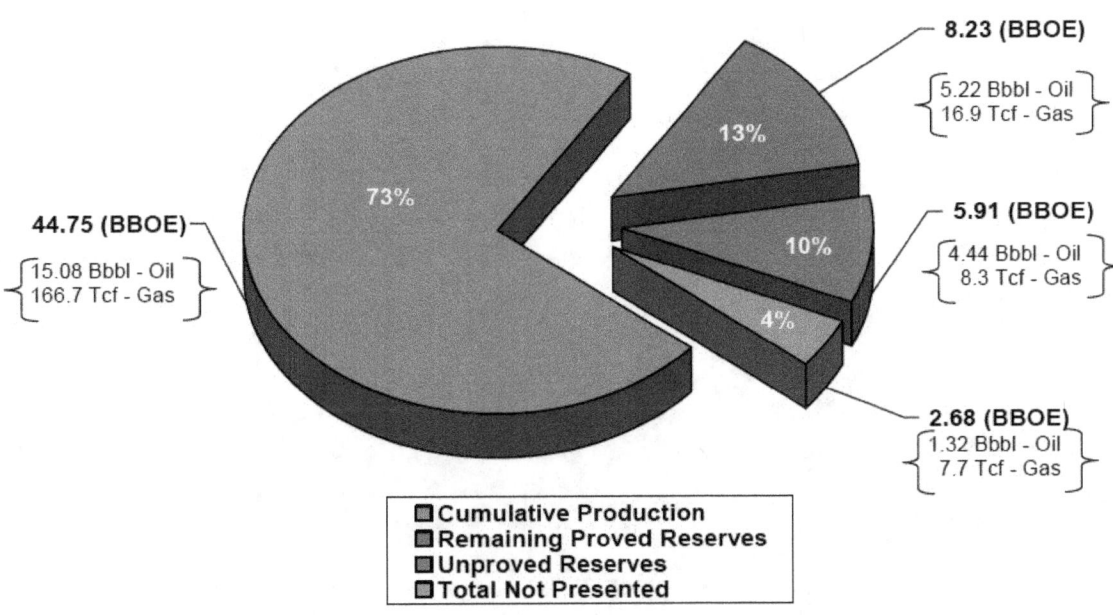

Gulf of Mexico Reserves and Resources

Introduction

This report, which supersedes the Minerals Management Service (MMS) OCS Report MMS 2009-022 (Crawford and others, 2009), presents estimated proved reserves, cumulative production, remaining proved reserves, and unproved reserves as of December 31, 2006, for the Gulf of Mexico (GOM). Reserves growth (an observed phenomenon that occurs when there is an incremental increase through time in the estimates of proved reserves) and undiscovered and known resources are not addressed in this report. A discussion of reserves growth can be found in OCS Report MMS 2001-0087 (Lore and others, 2001). The estimates of reserves for this report were completed in December 2008 and represent the combined efforts of engineers, geologists, geophysicists, paleontologists, and other personnel of the MMS Gulf of Mexico Region, Office of Resource Evaluation, in New Orleans, Louisiana.

As in previous reports, standard methods of estimating reserves were used, including volumetric calculations and performance analyses.

Definition of Resource and Reserve Terms

The MMS definitions and classification schema concerning reserves reflect those of the Society of Petroleum Engineers (SPE) and the World Petroleum Congress (WPC), 1996. SPE definitions have been used since 1988. The MMS definitions and classification schema concerning resources are modified as referenced by the U.S. Department of the Interior, 1989. The MMS petroleum resource and reserve classifications are presented in **Figures 1 and 2.**

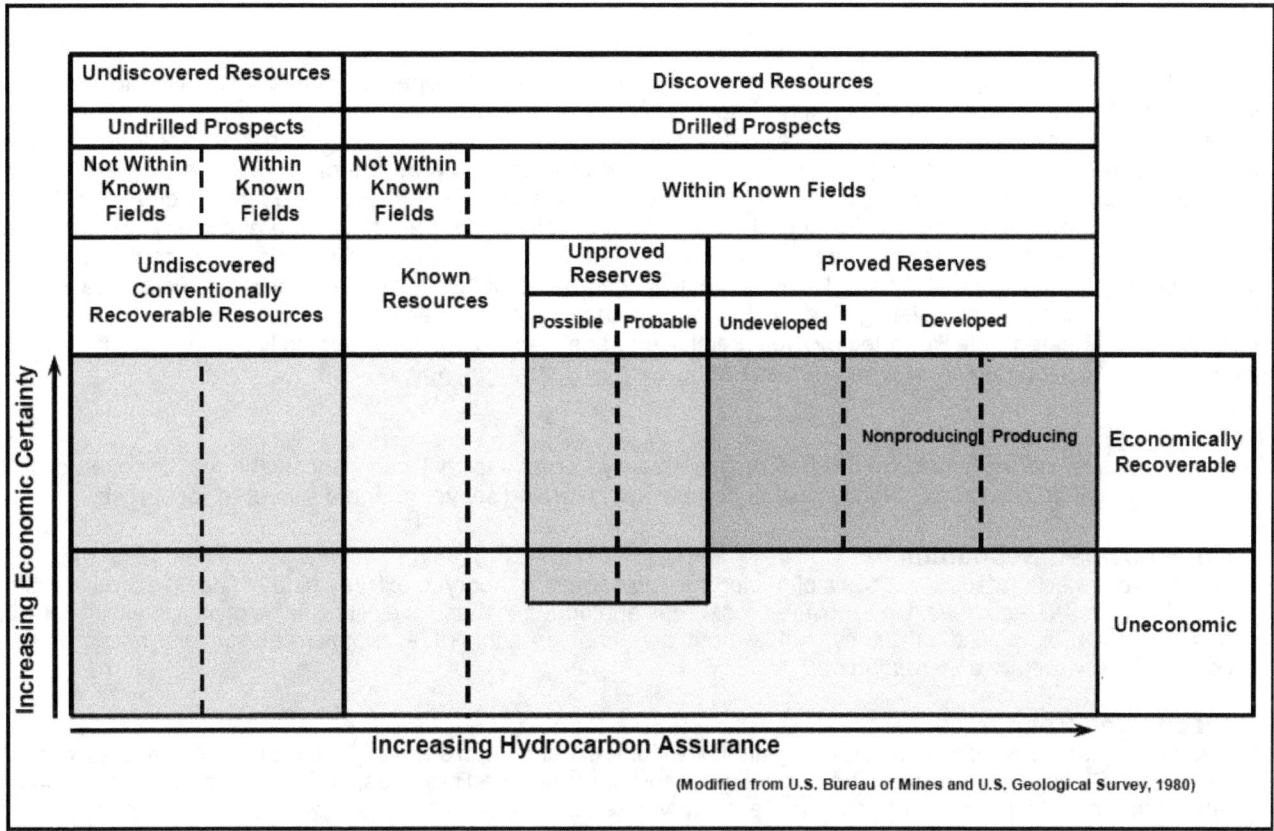

Figure 1. MMS conventionally recoverable petroleum resource classifications.

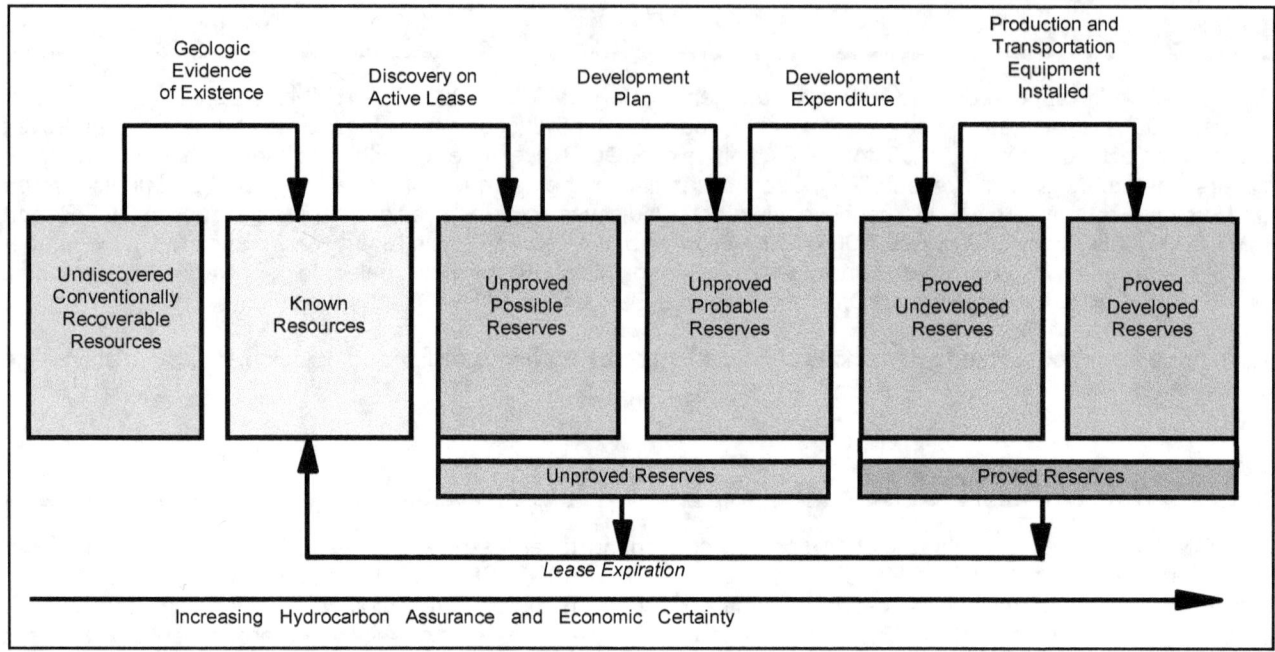

Figure 2. Gulf of Mexico MMS reserve classifications.

Field

A field is an area consisting of a single reservoir or multiple reservoirs all grouped on, or related to, the same general geologic structural feature and/or stratigraphic trapping condition. There may be two or more reservoirs in a field that are separated vertically by impervious strata, laterally by local geologic barriers, or by both. The area may include one OCS lease, a portion of an OCS lease, or a group of OCS leases with one or more wells that have been approved as producible by the MMS pursuant to the requirements of Title 30 Code of Federal Regulations (CFR) 250.115/116, Determination of Well Producibility. A field is usually named after the area and block on which the discovery well is located. Field names or field boundaries may be changed when additional geologic and/or production data initiate such a change. Using geological criteria, the MMS designates a new producible lease as a new field or assigns it to an existing field. A further explanation of field naming convention can be found in the "Reserves and Related Data Reported by Area" section on page 6 and in the Field Naming Handbook available from MMS's Gulf of Mexico Region Internet Web site at http://www.gomr.mms.gov.

Resources

Concentrations of naturally occurring liquid or gaseous hydrocarbons that can conceivably be discovered and recovered are called resources. Normal use encompasses both undiscovered and discovered resources.

Undiscovered Resources

Hydrocarbons estimated on the basis of geologic knowledge and theory to exist outside of known accumulations are *undiscovered resources.* Undiscovered resources analogous to those in existing fields producible with current recovery technology and efficiency, but without any consideration of economic viability, are *undiscovered conventionally recoverable resources.*

Discovered Resources

Hydrocarbons whose location and quantity are known or estimated from specific geologic evidence are *discovered resources.* Discovered resources include known resources, unproved reserves, and proved reserves depending upon economic, technical, contractual, or regulatory criteria.

Known Resources

Hydrocarbons associated with reservoirs penetrated by one or more wells that are on leases that are active, expired, relinquished, or terminated are identified as *known resources.*

Reserves

Those quantities of hydrocarbons which are anticipated to be recovered from known accumulations from a given date forward are reserves. All reserve estimates involve some degree of uncertainty. The uncertainty depends chiefly on the amount of reliable geologic and engineering data available at the time of the estimate and the interpretation of these data. The relative degree of uncertainty may be conveyed by placing reserves into one of two principal classifications, either unproved or proved.

Unproved Reserves

Those quantities of hydrocarbons that can be estimated with some certainty to be potentially recoverable from known reservoirs, assuming future economic conditions and technological developments, are *unproved reserves*. The MMS Gulf of Mexico Regional Field Names Committee designates a new producible lease as a new field or assigns it to an existing field. The reserves associated with new producible leases qualified pursuant to 30 CFR 250.115/116 are initially considered unproved reserves. Unproved reserves are less certain to be recovered than proved reserves and are further subclassified as possible and probable reserves to denote progressively increasing certainty in their recoverability. This report does not present individual estimates for possible and probable reserves.

> Unproved possible reserves are those unproved reserves which analysis of geological and engineering data suggests are less likely to be commercially recoverable than probable reserves. After a well on a lease qualifies, the reserves associated with the lease are initially classified as unproved possible because the only direct evidence of economic accumulations is a production test or electric log analysis.

> Unproved probable reserves are those unproved reserves which analysis of geological and engineering data suggests are more likely than not to be commercially recoverable. Fields that have a Development Operations Coordination Document (DOCD) on file with the MMS would be classified as unproved probable.

Proved Reserves

Those quantities of hydrocarbons which can be estimated with reasonable certainty to be commercially recoverable from known reservoirs under current economic conditions, operating methods, and government regulations are *proved reserves*. Establishment of current economic conditions includes consideration of relevant historical petroleum prices and associated costs and may involve an averaging period that is consistent with the purpose of the reserve estimate. Proved reserves must have either facilities operational at the time of the estimate to process and transport those reserves to market, or a commitment or reasonable expectation to install such facilities in the future. The application for a permit to install a platform is considered such a commitment. Proved reserves can be subdivided into undeveloped or developed.

> Proved undeveloped reserves exist where there is a relatively large expenditure required to install production and/or transportation facilities and a commitment has been made by the operator to develop the field. Proved undeveloped reserves are reserves expected to be recovered from planned development wells or from existing wells where a relatively large expenditure is required for field development.

> Proved developed reserves are expected to be recovered from existing wells (including reserves behind pipe). Reserves are considered developed only after the necessary production and transportation equipment has been installed, or when the costs to do so are relatively minor. Proved developed reserves are subcategorized as producing or nonproducing. This distinction is made at the reservoir level.

> > *Proved Developed Producing Reserves* are in reservoirs that have produced any time during the 12 months before the reporting date. Once the first reservoir in a field begins production, the reservoir and the field are considered proved developed producing.

> > *Proved Developed Nonproducing Reserves* are in reservoirs that have not produced during the 12 months prior to the reporting date. This category includes off-production reservoirs behind pipe and reservoirs awaiting workovers or transportation facilities. If all reservoirs in a field are off production, the field is considered proved developed nonproducing.

> Remaining proved reserves are the quantities of proved reserves currently estimated to be recoverable. Estimates of remaining proved reserves equal proved reserves minus cumulative production.

Reference Standard Conditions for Production and Reserves

Production data are the metered volumes of raw liquids and gas reported to the MMS by Federal unit and lease operators. Oil volume measurements and reserves are corrected to reference standard conditions of 60°F and one atmosphere (14.696 pounds per square inch absolute [psia]); gas measurements and reserves are corrected to 60°F and 15.025 psia. To convert gas volumes to 14.696 psia, multiply by 1.022 (DOE, 1989). Continuously measured volumes from production platforms and/or leases are allocated to individual wells and reservoirs on the basis of periodic well test gauges. These procedures introduce approximations in both production and remaining reserves data.

MMS Reporting of Reserve and Resource Data

OCS reserve estimates have been published by the Gulf of Mexico Region annually since 1977, presenting end-of-year totals starting with 1975. From 1977 to 1981, the estimates were published as United States Geological Survey (USGS) Open-File reports. The 1982 report was a joint publication between the USGS and the newly formed MMS, which assumed the OCS mission responsibilities at that time. The MMS has continued the reporting since 1983. The first report provided by MMS that also includes unproved reserve estimates was published in 1995.

Figure 3 shows the relationship of evaluated data to hydrocarbon assurance. The data are progressively aggregated on both a geologic and a geographic basis at each step of the evaluation process (the reservoir level through the region level). The most detailed studies of discovered resources are MMS individual field studies. These studies are based on analysis at the reservoir level (an example being a single fault trap in a single sand) and are used as the basis for the reporting of discovered and undiscovered resources. The geologic aggregation begins at the top of the figure at the reservoir level and progresses downward through the sand, pool, play, chronozone, series, and system to the region level. Reservoirs associated with a specific sand are aggregated to form the sand reporting level, which becomes the basis for further aggregations of data. A play is defined primarily (though not exclusively) by depositional style, geologic age at the chronozone level, and geographic area. Pools are based on the same characteristics as a play, but are specific to an individual field. Fields may contain one or more pools, with each pool representing a separate play. The geographic aggregation begins at the bottom of the figure, also at the reservoir level, and progresses upward through the field, area, and planning area to the region level.

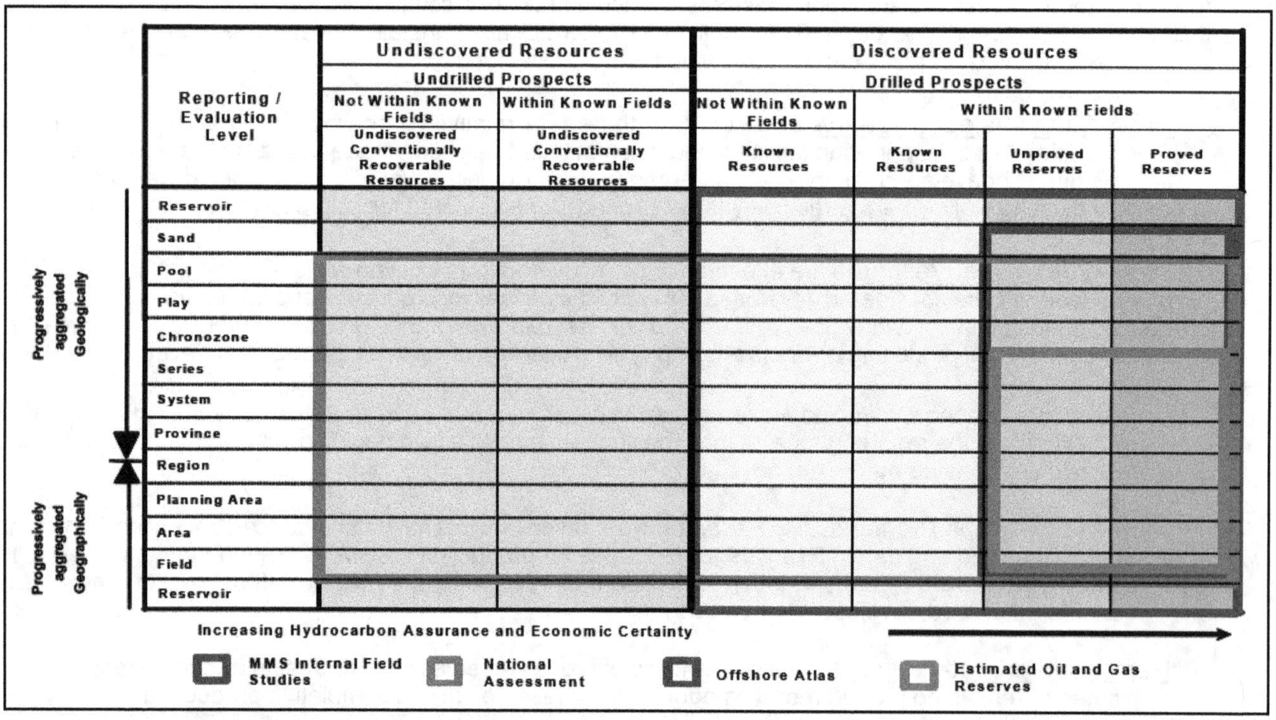

Figure 3. MMS evaluation of reserves and resources.

This report, *Estimated Oil and Gas Reserves*, presents reserve data for the field level through the series level (see **Figure 3**). This report is based on aggregation of MMS internal field studies completed at the reservoir and sand levels. All of the reservoir level data have been linked to the sand, pool, play, chronozone, and series level to support the Offshore Atlas Project (OAP).

The MMS OCS Report MMS 2001-086, *Atlas of Gulf of Mexico Gas and Oil Sands as of January 1, 1999*, provides a detailed geologic reporting of oil and gas proved and unproved reserves. Reserves data on more than 10,000 sands have been placed into 65 established geological plays in Federal waters. This is the second MMS release of a comprehensive framework of geologic and reserve data and the associated attributes for each specific sand and field. Play, chronozone, series, system, province, and region levels can also be evaluated with the data provided.

The MMS OCS Report MMS 2001-087, *2000 Assessment of Conventionally Recoverable Hydrocarbon Resources of the Gulf of Mexico and Atlantic Outer Continental Shelf as of January 1, 1999,* also known as the National Assessment, and it's update, *Assessment of Undiscovered Technically Recoverable Oil and Gas Resources of the Nation's Outer Continental Shelf, 2006,* address proved and unproved reserves, reserves appreciation, and undiscovered resources. To maintain credibility, an estimate of undiscovered resources must be based on discovered resources. The OAP supported this report by providing a framework of hydrocarbon plays that allowed for the logical extension of existing production rather than just a conceptual estimate. This report contains reserves and resource estimates by play, planning area, water depth, and region.

For information on these reports, contact the Gulf of Mexico Region's Public Information Office at 1-800-200-GULF or 504-736-2519, or visit MMS's Gulf of Mexico Region Internet Web site at http://www.gomr.mms.gov.

Methods Used for Estimating Reserves

Reserve estimates from geological and engineering analyses have been completed for the 1,229 proved fields. Reserves accountability is dependent on the drilling and development phases of fields. When a field is in the unproved category, geophysical mapping and limited well data are the basis for defining reservoir limits. Once a field is moved into the proved category and more data become available, the reserve estimate is re-evaluated. Well logs, well file data, seismic data, and production data are continually analyzed to improve the accuracy of the reserve estimate. As a field is depleted and/or abandoned, the proved reserves of productive reservoirs are assigned a value equal to the amount produced and the reserve estimate of non-producing reservoirs is converted to known resources. Currently, there are 273 proved expired, depleted fields.

Estimation of reserves is done under conditions of uncertainty. The method of estimation is called deterministic if the estimate is a single "best estimate" based on known geological, engineering, and economic data. The method of estimation is called probabilistic when the known geoscience, engineering, and economic data are used to generate a continuous range of estimates and their associated probabilities (SPE/AAPG/WPC/SPEE, 2007). Reserve estimates in this report are deterministic.

Methods used for estimating reserves can be categorized into three groups: analog, volumetric, and performance. The accuracy of the proved reserve estimate improves as more reservoir data become available to geoscientists and engineers. Resources are based on analogy with similar fields, reservoirs, or wells in the same area. Reserve estimates in this report are based primarily on volumetric and performance methods.

Analog

In the estimation of resources by analogy, geoscientists use seismic data to generate maps of the extent of subsurface formations. Estimates of undiscovered resources are based on analogy with similar fields, reservoirs, or wells in the same area before any wells have been drilled on a prospect. The seismic data help geoscientists identify prospects and resources, but do not provide enough direct data alone to estimate reserves.

The effective pore space, water saturation, net hydrocarbon thickness, pressure, volume, and temperature data, all necessary to complete resource estimates for prospects, come from nearby field and reservoir well data. After one or more wells are drilled and found producible, a volumetric estimate is done. These estimates, while incorporating existing data, still rely on some information obtained from analogs.

Volumetric

In a volumetric reserve estimate, data from drilled wells and seismic surveys are used to develop geologic interpretations. The effective pore space (porosity), water saturation, and net hydrocarbon thickness of the subsurface formations are calculated through evaluation of well logs, core analysis, and formation test data. Subsurface formations are mapped to determine area and net hydrocarbon thickness for each reservoir. Reservoir pressure, fluid volume, and temperature data from formation fluid samples are used to determine the change in volume of oil and gas that flow from higher pressure conditions deep underground to lower pressure conditions at the surface. All of these data are compiled, analyzed and applied to standard equations for the calculation of hydrocarbons in place within the reservoirs. Standard recovery factor equations are then applied to the in-place estimates to calculate proved and unproved reserves.

Performance Methods

In performance-technique methods, reserves are estimated by using mathematical or graphical techniques of production decline curve analysis and material balance. These techniques are used throughout the oil industry in assessing individual well, reservoir, or field performance and in forecasting future reserves. In decline analysis, a plot of daily production rate against time is most frequently used. Once a well or reservoir can no longer produce at its maximum capacity, the production rate declines. This production rate plotted against time can be extrapolated into the future to predict the remaining reserves. Another type of decline analysis is daily production rate plotted against cumulative production, which can also be used to predict remaining reserves. The declining daily rate is extrapolated to predict remaining reserves.

Another performance method, material balance, is used to estimate the amount of hydrocarbons in place. Given the premise that the pressure-volume relationship of a reservoir remains constant as hydrocarbons are produced, it is possible to equate expansion of reservoir fluids with reservoir voidage caused by fluid withdrawal minus any water influx. For depletion-drive gas reservoirs, a plot of the pressure/gas compressibility factor (P/Z) versus cumulative gas production provides an estimate of gas-in-place. Recoverable gas reserves are extrapolated to an abandonment reservoir pressure.

Reserves and Related Data Reported by Area

The Gulf of Mexico has been divided into three planning areas for administrative purposes; these planning areas as of December 31, 2006 (Western, Central, and Eastern) are shown in **Figures 4, 5,** and **6**, respectively. Each planning area is subdivided into protractions, which in turn are divided into numbered blocks. Fields in the Gulf of Mexico are identified by the protraction area name and block number of discovery – for example, East Cameron Block 271 Field.

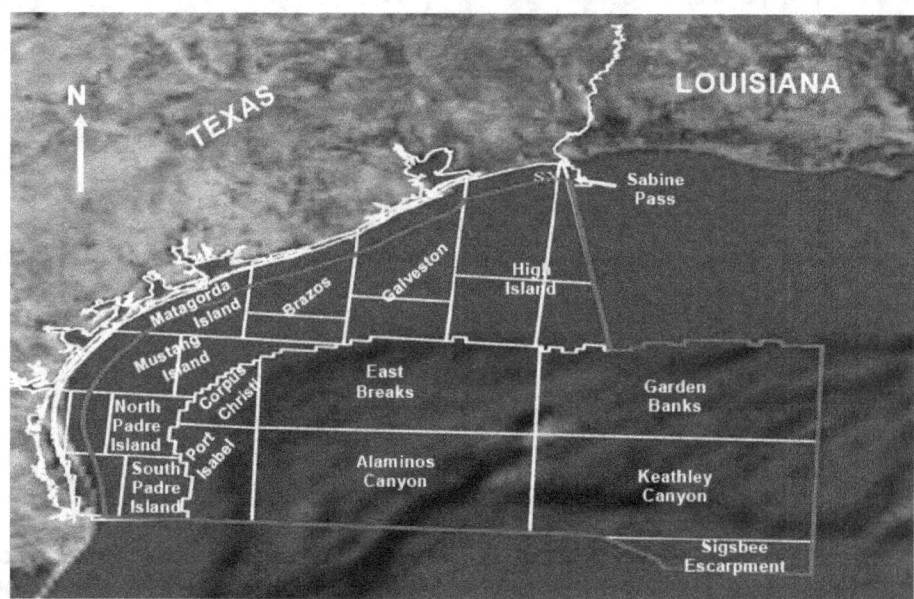

Figure 4. Western Planning Area, Gulf of Mexico, Outer Continental Shelf.

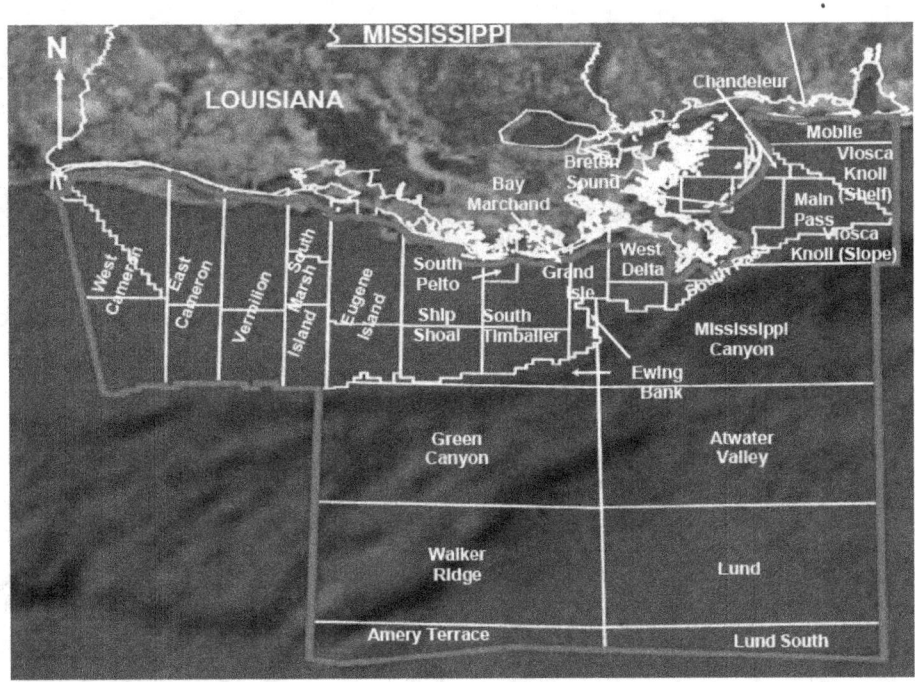

Figure 5. Central Planning Area, Gulf of Mexico, Outer Continental Shelf.

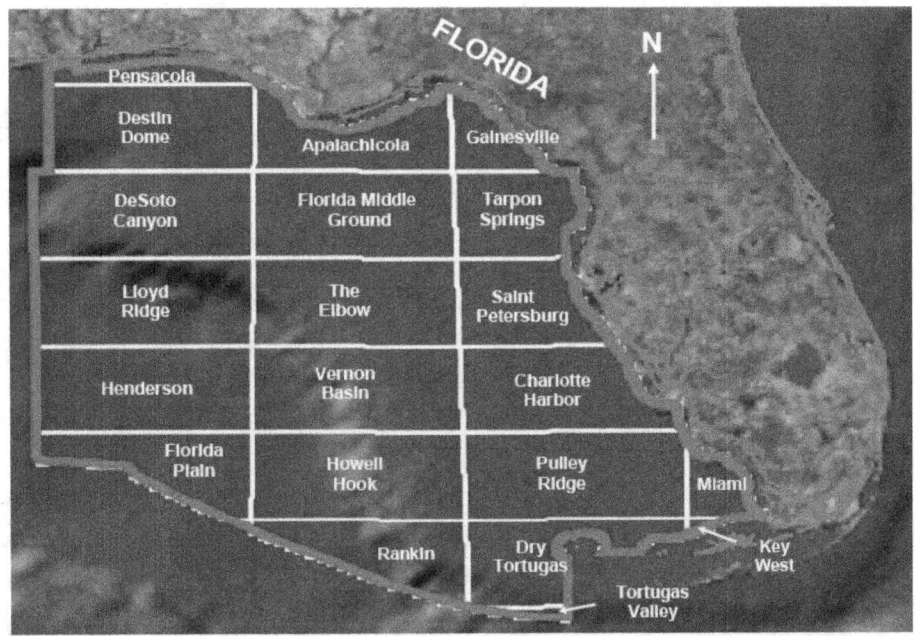

Figure 6. Eastern Planning Area, Gulf of Mexico, Outer Continental Shelf.

As the field is developed, the limits may expand into adjacent blocks and areas. These adjacent blocks are then identified as part of the original field and are given that field name. Statistics in this report are presented as area totals compiled under each field name. All of the data associated with East Cameron Block 271 Field are therefore included in the East Cameron totals, although part of the field extends into the adjacent area of Vermilion. There are four exceptions to the above field-naming techniques: Tiger Shoal and Lighthouse Point, included in South Marsh Island; Coon Point, included in Ship Shoal; and Bay Marchand, included in South Timbalier.

Through December 31, 2006, there were 1,015 proved and unproved active fields in the federally regulated part of the Gulf of Mexico. An updated list of the active and expired fields can be found in the *OCS Operations Field Directory* (updated monthly) available from MMS's Gulf of Mexico Region Internet Web site. There were 956 proved, active (producing and non-producing) fields and 59 unproved active fields studied. Included are the 273 proved expired, depleted fields, abandoned after producing 3.4 percent barrel oil equivalent of the total cumulative oil and gas production. Not studied were 91 fields expired, relinquished, or terminated without production. These fields may also be included in the *Indicated Hydrocarbon List* that can be found by visiting the MMS's Gulf of Mexico Region Internet Web site. In 2006, 28 proved fields expired including 22 proved fields that were depleted.

Reserves data and various classifications of fields, leases, boreholes, and completions are presented as area totals in **Tables 1** and **2**, and the **Table 3** series. (The **Table 3** series will be discussed in the section "Reserves Reported by Geologic Age," beginning on page 12.)

Table 1. Estimated oil and gas reserves for 1,229 proved fields and 59 unproved fields by area, Gulf of Mexico, Outer Continental Shelf, December 31, 2006.

(Reserves: oil expressed in millions of barrels at 60 °F and 1 atmosphere; gas in billions of cubic feet at 60 °F and 15.025 psia.)

Area(s) (Figs. 4, 5, and 6)	Number of fields						Proved reserves		Cumulative production through 2006		Remaining proved reserves		Unproved reserves	
	Proved active prod	Proved active nonprod	Proved expired depleted	Unproved active	studied	Expired nonprod	Oil	Gas	Oil	Gas	Oil	Gas	Oil	Gas
Western Planning Area														
Western Shelf														
Brazos	21	5	12	0	0	2	11	3,613	10	3,422	1	191	0	53
Galveston	23	4	21	0	0	3	71	2,234	55	1,963	16	271	0	48
High Island and Sabine Pass	70	9	48	1	1	9	400	15,497	381	14,882	19	615	8	278
Matagorda Island	22	0	6	0	0	3	24	5,241	22	4,987	2	254	1	317
Mustang Island	13	0	15	0	0	6	13	1,814	6	1,684	7	130	13	138
N & S.Padre Island	7	5	6	0	0	0	0	615	0	542	0	73	0	4
Western Slope														
Alaminos Canyon	3	1	0	3	3	2	346	452	61	98	285	354	130	275
East Breaks	17	2	0	2	2	4	237	2,360	175	1,604	62	756	16	89
Garden Banks	25	4	6	3	3	4	630	3,897	494	3,125	136	772	167	572
Western Slope (Other)*	0	0	0	2	2	1	0	0	0	0	0	0	1,350	301
Western Planning Area Subtotal	**201**	**30**	**114**	**11**	**11**	**34**	**1,732**	**35,723**	**1,204**	**32,307**	**528**	**3,416**	**1,685**	**2,075**
Central Planning Area														
Central Shelf														
Chandeleur	7	1	4	0	0	0	0	373	0	356	0	17	0	4
East Cameron	42	6	18	0	0	0	350	10,939	324	10,416	26	523	4	126
Eugene Island	68	10	9	0	0	3	1,647	19,541	1,586	18,790	61	751	36	225
Grand Isle	13	2	6	1	1	1	984	4,852	951	4,635	33	217	19	119
Main Pass and Breton Sound	53	10	21	5	5	5	1,119	6,693	1,029	6,176	90	517	6	94
Mobile	16	7	6	2	2	2	0	2,179	0	1,851	0	328	0	56
Ship Shoal	51	5	11	0	0	3	1,392	12,157	1,339	11,682	53	475	21	178
South Marsh Island	38	7	6	0	0	0	945	14,366	869	13,708	76	658	11	272
South Pass	7	4	2	0	0	1	1,083	4,357	1,051	4,220	32	137	1	7
South Pelto	9	0	0	0	0	0	159	1,201	149	1,056	10	145	4	14
South Timbalier	47	6	8	1	1	2	1,623	10,539	1,485	9,375	138	1,164	33	367
Vermilion	58	7	19	0	0	2	573	16,549	528	15,826	45	723	18	316
Viosca Knoll (Shelf)	16	0	14	2	2	1	12	472	11	419	1	53	0	17
West Cameron and Sabine Pass	78	13	26	0	0	0	224	20,749	203	19,392	21	1,357	10	402
West Delta	17	5	2	0	0	3	1,378	5,565	1,344	5,323	34	242	12	78
Central Slope														
Atwater Valley	0	4	0	5	5	3	51	407	0	0	51	407	108	313
Ewing Bank	14	2	0	0	0	2	312	500	241	382	71	118	52	103
Green Canyon	28	6	4	12	12	16	2,500	3,671	852	2,216	1,648	1,455	927	672
Mississippi Canyon	33	7	2	10	10	8	3,654	9,152	1,481	5,986	2,173	3,166	563	1,936
Viosca Knoll (Slope)	17	2	1	2	2	3	527	2,827	407	2,374	120	453	80	199
Central Slope (Other)**	1	0	0	6	6	0	29	173	26	158	3	15	851	163
Central Planning Area Subtotal	**613**	**104**	**159**	**46**	**46**	**55**	**18,562**	**147,262**	**13,876**	**134,341**	**4,686**	**12,921**	**2,756**	**5,661**
Eastern Planning Area Subtotal*	**2**	**6**	**0**	**2**	**2**	**2**	**1**	**676**	**0**	**93**	**1**	**583**	**0**	**539**
GOM Total:	**816** / **1,229**	**140**	**273**	**59**	**59**	**91**	**20,295**	**183,661**	**15,080**	**166,741**	**5,215**	**16,920**	**4,441**	**8,275**

*Western Slope (Other) includes Corpus Christi, Keathley Canyon, and Port Isabel.
**Central Slope (Other) includes Lund and Walker Ridge.
***Eastern Planning Area includes DeSoto Canyon, Destin Dome, Lloyd Ridge, and others.

Figure 7 provides a geographical representation of locations for the 1,229 proved fields in the Gulf of Mexico. The bar heights in the figure are proportional to total proved reserves (barrel of oil equivalent) for each proved field by decade.

Figure 8 provides a geographical representation of the 59 unproved active fields in the Gulf of Mexico. Estimates of unproved reserves are presented as planning area subtotals. The bar heights in the figure are proportional to total unproved reserves (barrel of oil equivalent) for each unproved field by decade.

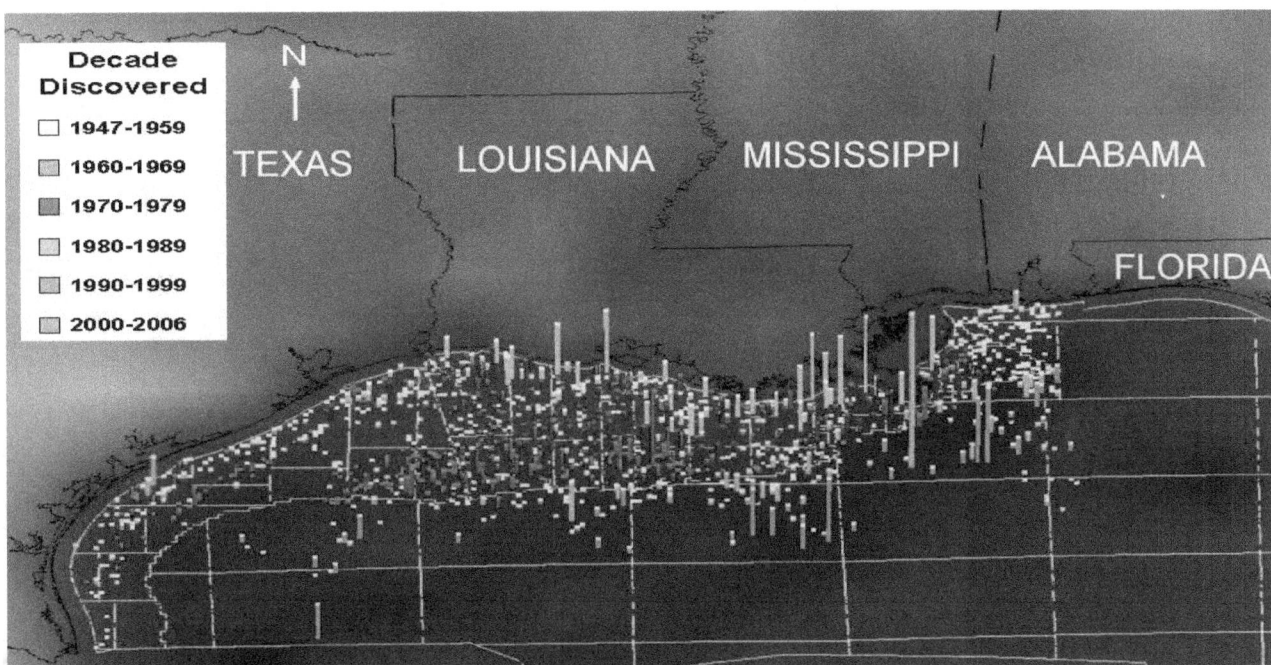

Figure 7. Gulf of Mexico, 1,229 proved fields (956 active and 273 depleted.)

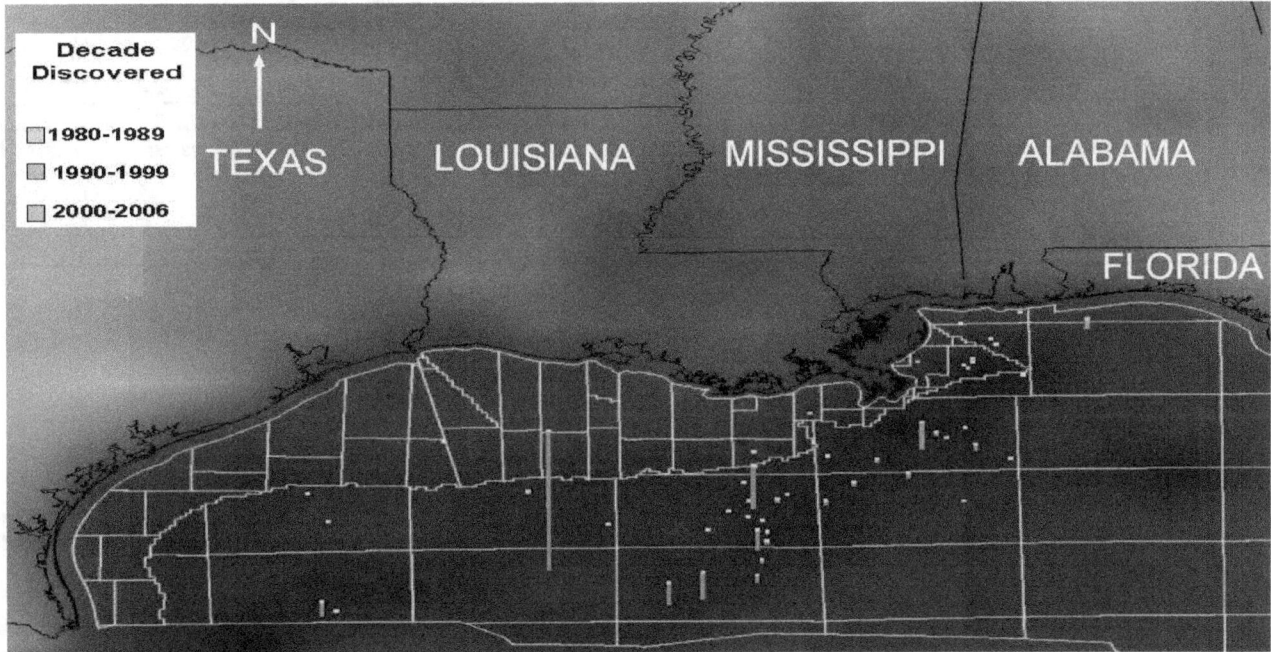

Figure 8. Gulf of Mexico, 59 unproved active fields.

9

Table 2. Status of oil and gas leases, boreholes, and completions by area, Gulf of Mexico, Outer Continental Shelf, December 31, 2006.

(All statistics associated with fields are presented within area totals compiled under each field name.)

Area(s) (Figs. 4, 5, and 6)	Number of leases					Number of boreholes		Number of active completions
	Proved active	Proved depleted	Unproved qualified	Unqualified active	Expired	Drilled	Abandoned	
Western Planning Area								
Western Shelf								
Brazos	37	58	0	58	360	594	446	165
Galveston	37	71	4	122	593	707	621	135
High Island and Sabine Pass	160	208	1	244	1,009	3,566	2,637	1,139
Matagorda Island	42	49	0	50	151	646	442	276
Mustang Island	27	35	0	51	422	469	361	151
N.& S.Padre Island	17	16	0	60	330	194	148	66
Western Slope								
Alaminos Canyon	12	3	3	438	263	53	31	10
East Breaks	35	10	0	316	475	372	245	131
Garden Banks	49	33	1	608	866	664	493	181
Western Slope (Other)*	7	1	3	701	345	25	23	0
Western Planning Area Subtotal	**423**	**484**	**12**	**2,648**	**4,814**	**7,290**	**5,447**	**2,254**
Central Planning Area								
Central Shelf								
Chandeleur	10	13	0	18	34	90	63	27
East Cameron	112	163	1	128	614	2,318	1,738	889
Eugene Island	219	143	2	124	481	5,568	3,965	1,992
Grand Isle	48	37	0	44	149	1,976	1,590	577
Main Pass and Breton Sound	141	125	8	101	398	3,206	2,029	1,479
Mobile	39	21	0	21	89	184	117	69
Ship Shoal	174	109	0	140	480	3,706	2,382	1,577
South Marsh Island	133	84	1	88	341	3,023	2,009	1,203
South Pass	39	26	0	22	98	2,368	1,535	1,062
South Pelto	22	5	0	4	30	422	293	187
South Timbalier	138	86	6	128	463	3,340	2,185	1,483
Vermilion	142	175	0	157	594	3,173	2,311	1,154
Viosca Knoll (Shelf)	67	40	0	102	358	608	385	162
West Cameron and Sabine Pass	215	284	1	276	956	3,794	2,837	1,310
West Delta	94	48	0	41	186	3,062	2,158	990
Central Slope								
Atwater Valley	7	4	1	371	374	95	79	13
Ewing Bank	28	16	0	69	245	366	263	111
Green Canyon	93	42	8	714	686	1,049	755	312
Mississippi Canyon	127	41	5	513	736	1,472	994	474
Viosca Knoll (Slope)	32	0	9	547	148	36	29	1
Central Slope (Other)**	32	0	9	547	148	36	29	22
Central Planning Area Subtotal	**1,912**	**1,462**	**51**	**4,155**	**7,608**	**39,892**	**27,746**	**15,094**
Eastern Planning Area Subtotal*	**5**	**8**	**86**	**155**	**349**	**83**	**67**	**11**
GOM Total:	**2,340**	**1,954**	**149**	**6,958**	**12,771**	**47,265**	**33,260**	**17,359**

*Western Slope (Other) includes Corpus Christi, Keathley Canyon, and Port Isabel.
**Central Slope (Other) includes Lund and Walker Ridge.
***Eastern Planning Area includes DeSoto Canyon, Destin Dome, Lloyd Ridge, and others.

The status of Gulf of Mexico OCS Federal oil and gas leases as of December 31, 2006, is presented in **Table 2**. There are 9,447 active leases (2,340 proved active, 149 unproved qualified, and 6,958 unqualified active) and 14,725 relinquished leases (1,954 proved depleted and 12,771 expired).

Definitions for the lease subgroups of **Table 2** are:

Proved Active — Leases within the designated 956 proved active fields presented in **Table 1**.

Proved Depleted — Leases relinquished after oil and gas production. The leases associated with the 273 depleted fields are represented here along with other produced, relinquished leases that are part of currently active fields.

Unproved Qualified — Leases associated with the 59 unproved active fields. The leases have qualified as producible under 30 CFR 250.115/116, but the operators have not established a commitment to produce. These fields may be classified as unproved possible or unproved probable.

Chronostratigraphy					Biostratigraphy		MMS Chronozone
Province	System	Subsystem	Series		Foraminifer & Ostracod (O)	Nannoplanktin	
			Holocene		Globorotalia inflata		
C e n o z o i c	Quaternary		Pleistocene	Upper	Globorotalia flexuosa Sangamon fauna	Emiliania huxleyi (base of acme) Gephyrocapsa oceanica (flood) Gephyrocapsa caribbeanica (flood)	PLU
				Middle	Trimosina "A"	Helicosphaera inversa Gephyrocapsa parallela Pseudoemiliania ovata	PLM
				Lower	Stilostomella antillea Trimosina "A" (acme) Hyalinea "B" / Trimosina "B" Angulogerina "B" Uvigerina hispida	Pseudoemiliania lacunosa "C" (acme) Calcidiscus macintyrei	PLL
	Tertiary	Neocene	Pliocene	Upper	Globorotalia crassula (acme) Lenticulina 1 Globoquadrina altispira Textularia 1	Discoaster brouweri	PU
				Lower	Buccella hannai (acme) Buliminella 1 Globorotalia plesiotumida (acme)	Sphenolithus abies Sphenolithus abies "B" Discoaster quintatus	PL
			Miocene	Upper	Globorotalia menardii (coiling change right-to-left) Textularia "X" Robulus "E" Bigenerina "A" Cristellaria "K" Bolivina thalmanni	Discoaster quinqueramus Discoaster berggrenii "A" Minylithus convallis Catinaster mexicanus Discoaster prepentaradiatus (increase)	MUU
					Discorbis 12 Bigenerina 2 Uvigerina 3	Helicosphaera walbersdorfensis Coccolithus miopelagicus	MLU
				Middle	Globorotalia fohsi robusta Textularia "W" Globorotalia peripheroacuta	Discoaster kugleri Discoaster kugleri (acme) Discoaster sanmiguelensis (increase)	MUM
					Bigenerina humblei Cristellaria "I" Cibicides opima	Sphenolithus heteromorphus Sphenolithus heteromorphus (acme)	MMM
					Cristellaria / Robulus / Lenticulina 53 Amphistegina "B" Robulus 43 Cibicides 38	Helicosphaera ampliaperta Discoaster deflandrei (acme) Discoaster calculosus	MLM
				Lower	Cristellaria 54 / Eponides 14 Gyroidina "K" Catapsydrax stainforthi	Reticulofenestra gartneri Sphenolithus disbelemnos	MUL
					Discorbis "B" Marginulina "A"	Orthorhabdus serratus Triquetrorhabdulus carinatus	MML
					Siphonina davisi Lenticulina hanseni	Discoaster saundersi Helicosphaera recta	MLL
		Paleogene	Oligocene	Upper	Robulus "A" Heterostegina texana Camerina "A" Bolivina mexicana	Dictyococcites bisectus Sphenolithus delphix	OU
				Lower	Nonion struma Textularia warreni	Sphenolithus pseudoradians Ismolithus recurvus	OL
			Eocene	Upper	Hantkenina alabamensis Camerina moodybranchensis	Discoaster saipanensis Cribrocentrum reticulatum Sphenolithus obtusus	EU
				Middle	Nonionella cockfieldensis Discorbis yeguaensis	Micrantholithus procerus Pemma basquensis Discoaster lodoensis	EM
				Lower	Globorotalia wilcoxensis	Chiasmolithus californicus Toweius crassus Discoaster multiradiatus	EL
			Paleocene	Upper	Morozovella velascoensis Vaginulina longiforma Vaginulina midwayana	Fasciculithus tympaniformis	LU
				Lower	Globorotalia trinidadensis Globigerina eugubina	Chiasmolithus danicus	LL
M e s o z o i c	Cretaceous	Upper	Gulfian		Abathomphalus mayaroensis Rosita fornicata Dicarinella concavata Hedbergella amabilis	Micula decussata Micula prinsii FAD Lithastrinus moratus Stoverius achylosus	KUU
					Dicarinella hagni Planulina eaglefordensis Rotalipora cushmani Favusella washitaensis Rotalipora gandolfii	Lithraphidites acutus	KLU
		Lower	Comanchean		Cythereis fredericksburgensis (O) Ammobaculites goodlandensis	Hayesites albiensis Braarudosphaera hockwoldensis	KUL
					Dictyoconus walnutensis Eocytheropteron trinitiensis (O) Orbitolina texana Rehacythereis? aff. R. glabrella (O)	Rucinolithus irregularis	KML
			Coahuilan		Ticinella bejaouaensis Choffatella decipiens Schuleridea acuminata (O)	Diadorhombus rectus Polycostella beckmanni	KLL
	Jurassic		Upper		Gallaecytheridea postrotunda (O) Epistomina uhligi Epistomina mosquensis Alveosepta jaccardi Paalzowella feifeli	Stephanolithion bigotii bigotii Stephanolithion bigotii maximum Stephanolithion speciosum	JU
			Middle		Reinholdella crebra	Watznaueria crucicentralis	JM

Abbreviated MMS Gulf of Mexico biostratigraphic chart illustrating chronostratigraphy, biostratigraphy, and MMS chronozones codes. For the complete chart visit http /www.gomr.mms.gov/homepg/whatsnew/papers/biochart.pdf.

Figure 9. Gulf of Mexico geologic time scale.

Unqualified Active — Active exploratory leases not yet qualified as producible or associated with any field.

Expired — Leases expired, terminated, or relinquished by the operator without having produced any oil or gas, although some were once qualified as producible under 30 CFR 250.115/116. There are 91 expired fields with no production.

The total number of boreholes drilled and the number of boreholes plugged and abandoned are also shown in **Table 2**. There were 760 boreholes spudded during 2006, compared with 816 during 2005, and 897 during 2004. The last column of **Table 2** presents the total number of active completions per area. Active completions are defined as those with perforations open to the formation and not isolated by permanent plugs; service wells (injection, disposal, or water source) are included. The presence or absence of production or injection is not considered. The number of boreholes and the number of active completions listed in this report are based on reports received by the MMS at the time the count was made in 2009. These numbers may change as data are received, processed, and edited.

Reserves Reported by Geologic Age

In this report, the 1,229 proved and 59 unproved fields have been classified at the geologic series level. The different geologic age classifications currently in use by MMS are shown in Figure 9. Paleontological examinations of borehole cuttings, along with regional analysis of geological and geophysical data, were used in determining the age classifications. Hundreds of additional foraminiferal and nannofossil bioevents were incorporated into an update of the MMS Biostratigraphic Chart (www.gomr.mms.gov/homepg/whatsnew/papers/biochart.pdf) to aid in geologic mapping, stratigraphic correlation, and paleobathymetric zonation. Using standardized global stratigraphic concepts, this new version of the chart incorporates the latest information currently used as biostratigraphic datum markers by industry paleontologists for the Mesozoic and Cenozoic geologic provinces. This biostratigraphic chart update reduces the disjoint between the industry/academia biostratigraphic naming convention and the MMS-standard chronozone naming convention, hence MMS reserves allocations.

Table 3 shows the distribution of reserves and production data by geologic age and planning area. **Tables 3a** through **3e** also show the distribution of reserves and production data by geologic age, but further subdivide the planning areas as area totals. Please note that this report contains the term "Span Ages," which is used to denote a geologic age classification that spans more than one series (see **Tables 3** and **3e**).

Table 3. Estimated oil and gas reserves for 1,229 proved and 59 unproved fields by geologic age, Gulf of Mexico, Outer Continental Shelf, December 31, 2006.

(Reserves: oil expressed in millions of barrels at 60 °F and 1 atmosphere, gas in billions of cubic feet at 60 °F and 15 025 psia)

Area	Number of proved reservoirs	Proved reserves		Cumulative production through 2006		Remaining proved reserves		Number of unproved reservoirs	Unproved reserves	
		Oil	Gas	Oil	Gas	Oil	Gas		Oil	Gas
Western Planning Area										
Pleistocene	1,132	266	7,843	213	7,393	53	450	141	40	248
Pliocene	873	951	8,320	795	6,993	156	1,327	126	125	457
Miocene	2,499	243	19,197	196	17,899	47	1,298	222	41	800
Pre-Miocene	8	0	35	0	22	0	13	0	0	0
Span Ages	8	272	328	0	0	272	328	14	1,479	570
Western Planning Area Subtotal	*4,520*	*1,732*	*35,723*	*1,204*	*32,307*	*528*	*3,416*	*503*	*1,685*	*2,075*
Central Planning Area										
Pleistocene	3,557	1,118	20,531	1,032	19,525	86	1,006	318	72	462
Pliocene	9,624	6,089	48,480	5,325	45,642	764	2,838	741	232	1,220
Miocene	11,471	10,024	75,348	7,488	67,382	2,536	7,966	929	732	3,155
Pre-Miocene	37	0	2,096	0	1,778	0	318	8	0	64
Span Ages	45	1,331	807	31	14	1,300	793	57	1,720	760
Central Planning Area Subtotal	*24,734*	*18,562*	*147,262*	*13,876*	*134,341*	*4,686*	*12,921*	*2,053*	*2,756*	*5,661*
Eastern Planning Area										
Miocene	17	1	676	0	93	1	583	7	0	48
Pre-Miocene	0	0	0	0	0	0	0	1	0	491
Eastern Planning Area Subtotal	*17*	*1*	*676*	*0*	*93*	*1*	*583*	*8*	*0*	*539*
GOM Total	29,271	20,295	183,661	15,080	166,741	5,215	16,920	2,564	4,441	8,275

Data from **Table 3a** were used to generate the Pleistocene reserves trend presented in **Figure 10** and correspond to the *Globorotalia flexuosa* through *Uvigerina hispida* biozones. Production within the Pleistocene extends from the Galveston area to east of the modern-day mouth of the Mississippi River. Pleistocene productive sands are limited in the east and west because of a lack of sediment influx at the edge of the depocenter. Deepwater Pleistocene production occurs in the East Breaks through Mississippi Canyon areas, and well control suggests sands continue beyond the Sigsbee Escarpment. Through December 31, 2006, the Pleistocene produced from 402 fields. Proved reserves were 1.38 billion barrels (Bbbl) and 28.4 trillion cubic feet (Tcf). Remaining proved reserves were 0.14 Bbbl and 1.5 Tcf.

Table 3a. Estimated oil and gas reserves for Pleistocene reservoirs in 402 proved and 7 unproved fields by area, Gulf of Mexico, Outer Continental Shelf, December 31, 2006.

(Reserves: oil expressed in millions of barrels at 60 °F and 1 atmosphere, gas in billions of cubic feet at 60 °F and 15 025 psia)

Area	Number of proved reservoirs	Proved reserves		Cumulative production through 2006		Remaining proved reserves		Number of unproved reservoirs	Unproved reserves	
		Oil	Gas	Oil	Gas	Oil	Gas		Oil	Gas
Western Planning Area										
Alaminos Canyon	0	0	0	0	0	0	0	1	0	5
East Breaks	32	10	201	7	148	3	53	3	0	7
Galveston	3	0	17	0	15	0	2	0	0	0
Garden Banks	115	112	1,364	69	1,182	43	182	60	38	153
High Island and Sabine Pass	967	144	6,217	137	6,039	7	178	76	2	79
N & S Padre Island	15	0	45	0	9	0	35	1	0	4
Western Slope (Other)*	0	0	0	0	0	0	0	0	0	0
Western Planning Area Subtotal	*1,132*	*266*	*7,844*	*213*	*7,393*	*53*	*450*	*141*	*40*	*248*
Central Planning Area										
Atwater Valley	0	0	0	0	0	0	0	1	0	22
East Cameron	358	200	1,496	185	1,354	15	142	44	2	33
Eugene Island	862	330	5,633	312	5,532	18	101	24	2	19
Ewing Bank	64	36	217	29	181	7	37	19	24	55
Grand Isle	34	0	91	0	82	0	10	4	0	2
Green Canyon	146	87	564	75	484	12	80	50	12	54
Main Pass and Breton Sound	5	0	16	0	16	0	0	0	0	0
Mississippi Canyon	28	5	684	5	588	0	96	10	8	19
Ship Shoal	276	68	1,785	65	1,756	3	29	12	1	9
South Marsh Island	438	243	1,885	227	1,804	16	81	32	3	50
South Pass	26	1	240	1	240	0	0	0	0	0
South Pelto	9	0	10	0	6	0	4	0	0	0
South Timbalier	210	46	990	43	920	3	70	13	2	15
Vermilion	533	80	1,761	72	1,637	8	124	46	12	94
Viosca Knoll (Slope)	2	0	28	0	28	0	28	0	0	0
West Cameron and Sabine Pass	540	22	4,982	18	4,794	4	187	60	6	90
West Delta	26	0	148	0	131	0	17	3	0	0
Central Slope (O her)**	0	0	0	0	0	0	0	0	0	0
Central Planning Area Subtotal	*3,557*	*1,118*	*20,530*	*1,032*	*19,525*	*86*	*1,006*	*318*	*72*	*462*
*Eastern Planning Area Subtotal***	*0*	*0*	*0*	*0*	*0*	*0*	*0*	*0*	*0*	*0*
GOM Total	**4,689**	**1,384**	**28,374**	**1,245**	**26,918**	**139**	**1,456**	**459**	**112**	**710**

*Western Slope (Other) includes Corpus Christi, Keathley Canyon, and Port Isabel.
**Central Slope (Other) includes Lund and Walker Ridge.
***Eastern Planning Area includes DeSoto Canyon, Destin Dome, Lloyd Ridge, and others.

Data from **Table 3b** were used to generate the Pliocene reserves trend presented in **Figure 11** and correspond to *the Globorotalia crassula (acme)* through *Globorotalia plesiotumida (acme)* biozones. Production within the Pliocene extends from south of Galveston in the west to south of Mobile Bay in the east. Pliocene deepwater production extends extend into the areas of East Breaks, Garden Banks, Green Canyon, Ewing Bank, and Mississippi Canyon. Well control suggests Pliocene sands extend at least as far as the Sigsbee Escarpment. Through December 31, 2006, the Pliocene produced from 541 fields. Proved reserves were 7.00 Bbbl and 56.8 Tcf. Remaining proved reserves were 0.92 Bbbl and 4.2 Tcf.

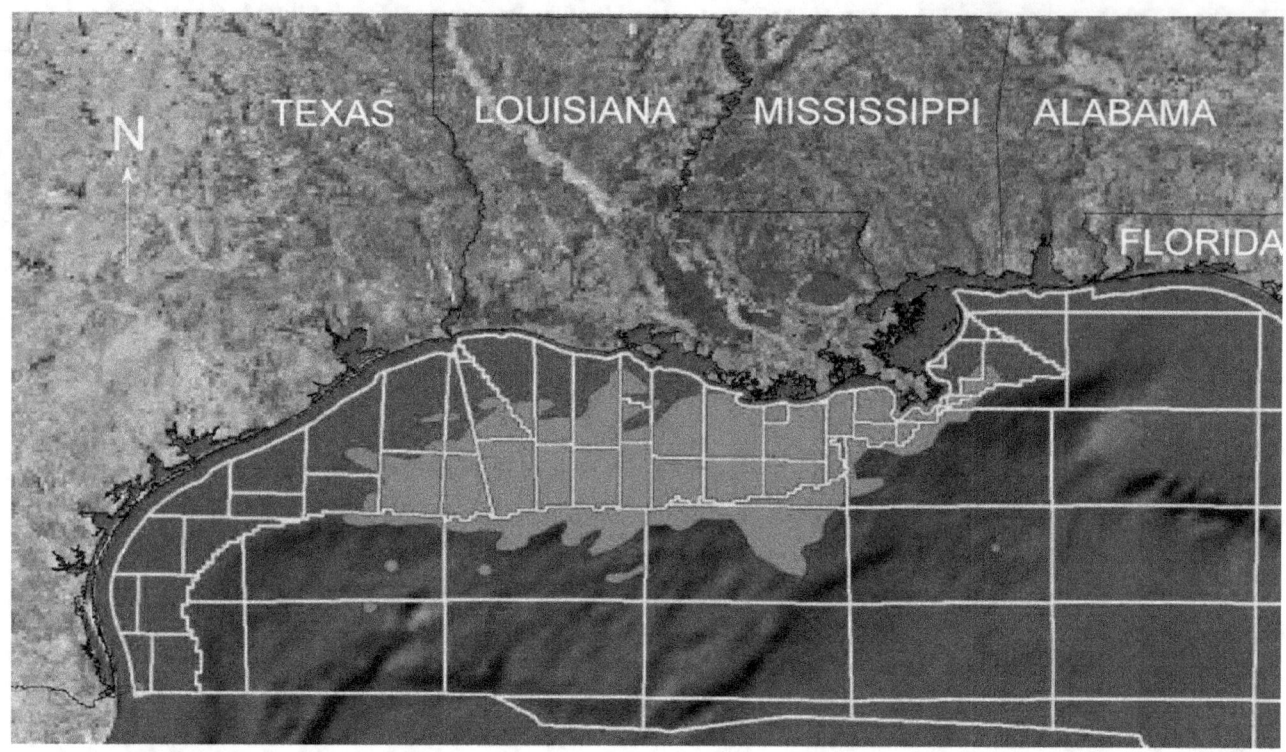

Figure 10. Pleistocene reserves trend.

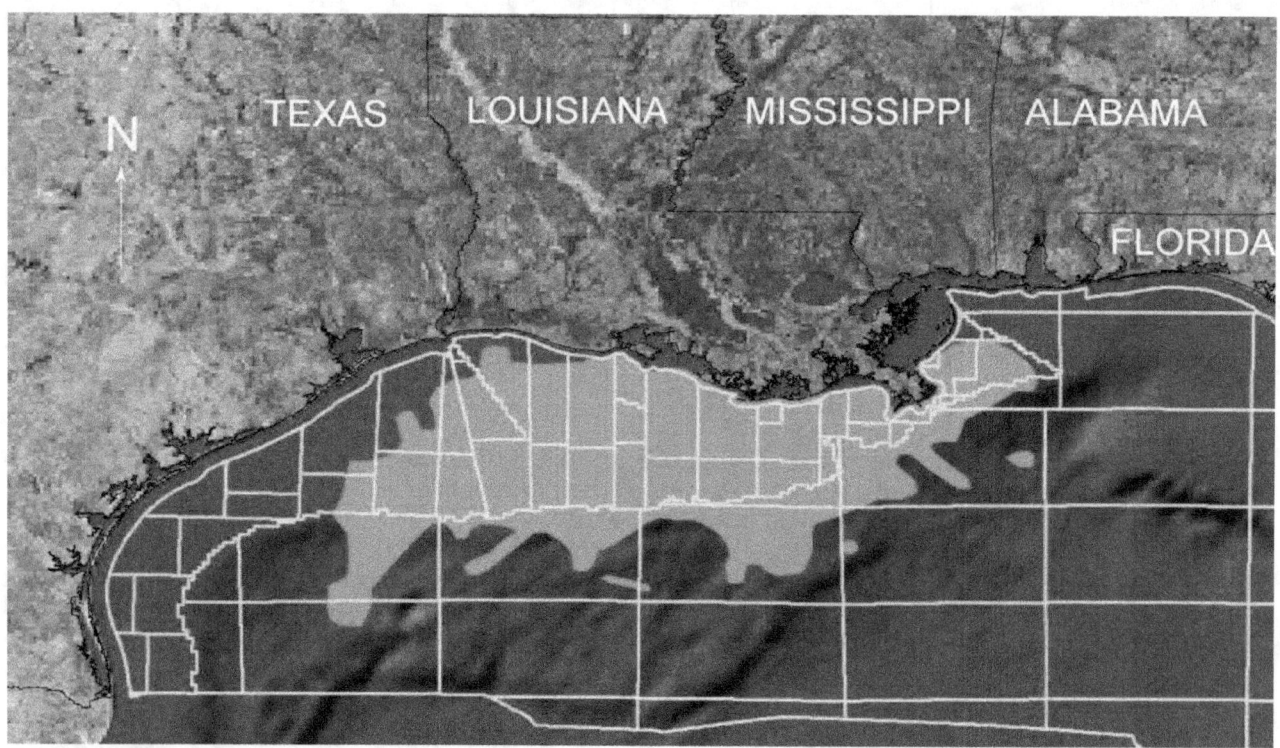

Figure 11. Pliocene reserves trend.

Table 3b. Estimated oil and gas reserves for Pliocene reservoirs in 541 proved and 15 unproved fields by area, Gulf of Mexico, Outer Continental Shelf, December 31, 2006.

(Reserves: oil expressed in millions of barrels at 60 °F and 1 atmosphere, gas in billions of cubic feet at 60 °F and 15 025 psia)

Area	Number of proved reservoirs	Proved reserves		Cumulative production through 2006		Remaining proved reserves		Number of unproved reservoirs	Unproved reserves	
		Oil	Gas	Oil	Gas	Oil	Gas		Oil	Gas
Western Planning Area										
Alaminos Canyon	2	63	116	53	92	10	24	0	0	0
East Breaks	142	226	1,830	167	1,200	59	630	28	16	82
Galveston	20	1	70	1	70	0	0	0	0	0
Garden Banks	89	455	2,276	379	1,749	76	527	50	106	327
High Island and Sabine Pass	620	205	4,028	196	3,882	9	146	48	3	47
Western Slope (Other)*	0	0	0	0	0	0	0	0	0	0
Western Planning Area Subtotal	*873*	*950*	*8,320*	*796*	*6,993*	*154*	*1,327*	*126*	*125*	*456*
Central Planning Area										
Atwater Valley	0	0	0	0	0	0	0	4	14	16
East Cameron	571	70	4,843	64	4,659	6	184	59	2	58
Eugene Island	1,520	882	7,803	858	7,596	24	207	127	14	61
Ewing Bank	54	243	242	190	175	53	67	16	14	37
Grand Isle	197	43	1,828	41	1,780	2	48	16	2	13
Green Canyon	197	1,054	2,210	706	1,667	348	543	81	92	216
Main Pass and Breton Sound	120	70	726	59	701	11	25	1	0	1
Mississippi Canyon	269	549	2,733	419	2,497	130	236	60	52	338
Ship Shoal	1,808	1,037	7,332	1,002	7,046	35	286	101	8	85
South Marsh Island	705	375	3,589	337	3,339	38	250	48	5	50
South Pass	802	541	2,342	528	2,261	13	81	8	0	5
South Pelto	145	49	57	48	55	1	2	2	2	7
South Timbalier	1,086	406	4,991	364	4,624	42	367	115	12	206
Vermilion	867	265	4,262	240	4,056	25	206	47	3	65
Viosca Knoll (Slope)	23	55	110	36	87	19	23	2	3	3
West Cameron and Sabine Pass	667	30	4,056	27	3,837	3	219	35	2	41
West Delta	539	392	1,183	379	1,104	13	79	16	7	15
Central Slope (O her)**	54	29	173	26	158	3	15	3	0	4
Central Planning Area Subtotal	*9,624*	*6,090*	*48,480*	*5,324*	*45,642*	*766*	*2,838*	*741*	*232*	*1,221*
Eastern Planning Area Subtotal*	*0*	*0*	*0*	*0*	*0*	*0*	*0*	*0*	*0*	*0*
GOM Total	10,497	7,040	56,800	6,120	52,635	920	4,165	867	357	1,677

*Western Slope (Other) includes Corpus Christi, Keathley Canyon, and Port Isabel.
**Central Slope (Other) includes Lund and Walker Ridge.
***Eastern Planning Area includes DeSoto Canyon, Destin Dome, Lloyd Ridge, and others.

Data from **Table 3c** were used to generate the Miocene reserves trend presented in **Figure 12** and correspond to the *Globorotalia menardii (coiling change right-to-left)* through *Lenticulina hanseni* biozones. Production within the Miocene extends from North Padre Island in the west to east of the Mississippi River. Miocene productive sands also extend into deepwater from East Breaks and Garden Banks in the west to Ewing Bank, Green Canyon, Viosca Knoll, Mississippi Canyon, Atwater Valley, Destin Dome, Desoto Canyon, and Lloyd Ridge in the east. Wells indicate sands continue beyond the Sigsbee Escarpment. Through December 31, 2006 the Miocene produced from 718 fields. Proved reserves were 10.27 Bbbl and 95.2 Tcf. Remaining proved reserves were 2.58 Bbbl and 9.8 Tcf.

Data from **Table 3d** were used to generate the Pre-Miocene reserves trend presented in **Figure 13** and include the Oligocene, Eocene, and Paleocene in the Tertiary series, and the Cretaceous and Jurassic series. These reservoirs include Jurassic Norphlet sands and Lower Cretaceous Carbonates. Production within the Jurassic is limited to east of the Mississippi River in the Mobile area. Well control suggests reservoir sands continuing eastward into Destin Dome. Through December 31, 2006, these trends produced from 24 fields. Proved reserves were less than 0.01 Bbbl and 2.2 Tcf. Remaining proved reserves were less than 0.01 Bbbl and 0.4 Tcf.

Data from **Table 3e** were used to generate reserves for the reservoirs in fields that span ages from Upper Pleistocene to the Lower Paleogene. Proved reserves were 1.6 Bbbl and 1.1 Tcf.

Table 3c. Estimated oil and gas reserves for Miocene reservoirs in 718 proved and 15 unproved fields by area, Gulf of Mexico, Outer Continental Shelf, December 31, 2006.

(Reserves: oil expressed in millions of barrels at 60 °F and 1 atmosphere, gas in billions of cubic feet at 60 °F and 15.025 psia)

Area	Number of proved reservoirs	Proved reserves		Cumulative production through 2006		Remaining proved reserves		Number of unproved reservoirs	Unproved reserves	
		Oil	Gas	Oil	Gas	Oil	Gas		Oil	Gas
Western Planning Area										
Alaminos Canyon	1	11	7	9	6	2	1	0	0	0
Brazos	438	11	3,613	10	3,422	1	191	41	0	53
East Breaks	5	1	329	1	256	0	73	0	0	0
Galveston	407	68	2,147	53	1,878	15	269	31	0	48
Garden Banks	7	64	257	47	194	17	63	9	24	93
High Island and Sabine Pass	707	51	5,253	48	4,961	3	292	48	3	151
Matagorda Island	476	25	5,240	23	4,987	2	253	63	1	317
Mustang Island	341	12	1,780	5	1,662	7	118	28	13	137
N.& S.Padre Island	117	0	571	0	533	0	38	2	0	1
Western Slope (Other)*	0	0	0	0	0	0	0	0	0	0
Western Planning Area Subtotal	*2,499*	*243*	*19,197*	*196*	*17,899*	*47*	*1,298*	*222*	*41*	*800*
Central Planning Area										
Atwater Valley	11	1	359	0	0	1	359	7	18	46
Chandeleur	30	0	373	0	356	0	17	5	0	4
East Cameron	422	80	4,600	75	4,403	5	197	21	0	35
Eugene Island	1,323	436	6,105	416	5,661	20	444	150	19	143
Ewing Bank	15	35	42	23	26	12	16	6	15	17
Grand Isle	732	940	2,933	909	2,773	31	159	102	18	104
Green Canyon	16	79	137	41	51	38	86	18	30	29
Main Pass and Breton Sound	1,480	1,049	5,950	970	5,459	79	491	19	6	93
Mississippi Canyon	185	3,099	5,734	1,057	2,900	2,042	2,834	95	503	1,579
Mobile	38	0	391	0	341	0	50	3	0	9
Ship Shoal	841	288	3,041	271	2,881	17	160	49	11	85
South Marsh Island	912	328	8,892	305	8,565	23	327	79	3	172
South Pass	569	541	1,775	522	1,719	19	56	4	1	2
South Pelto	420	109	1,133	100	994	9	139	8	2	7
South Timbalier	1,196	1,170	4,559	1,079	3,832	91	727	90	19	145
Vermilion	1,000	227	10,526	215	10,134	12	392	89	3	156
Viosca Knoll (Shelf)	33	12	173	11	160	1	13	2	0	0
Viosca Knoll (Slope)	107	473	2,689	372	2,287	101	402	22	77	196
West Cameron and Sabine Pass	1,221	171	11,703	156	10,752	15	951	120	2	270
West Delta	920	986	4,233	966	4,088	20	146	40	5	63
Central Slope (Other)**	0	0	0	0	0	0	0	0	0	0
Central Planning Area Subtotal	*11,471*	*10,024*	*75,348*	*7,488*	*67,382*	*2,536*	*7,966*	*929*	*732*	*3,155*
*Eastern Planning Area Subtotal***	*17*	*1*	*676*	*0*	*93*	*1*	*583*	*7*	*0*	*48*
GOM Total	**13,987**	**10,268**	**95,221**	**7,684**	**85,374**	**2,584**	**9,847**	**1,158**	**773**	**4,003**

*Western Slope (Other) includes Corpus Christi, Keathley Canyon, and Port Isabel.
**Central Slope (Other) includes Lund and Walker Ridge.
***Eastern Planning Area includes DeSoto Canyon, Destin Dome, Lloyd Ridge, and others.

Table 3d. Estimated oil and gas reserves for Pre-Miocene reservoirs in 24 proved and 3 unproved fields by area, Gulf of Mexico, Outer Continental Shelf, December 31, 2006.

(Reserves: oil expressed in millions of barrels at 60 °F and 1 atmosphere, gas in billions of cubic feet at 60 °F and 15.025 psia)

Area	Number of proved reservoirs	Proved reserves		Cumulative production through 2006		Remaining proved reserves		Number of unproved reservoirs	Unproved reserves	
		Oil	Gas	Oil	Gas	Oil	Gas		Oil	Gas
Western Planning Area										
Mustang Island and N. & S. Padre	8	0	35	0	22	0	13	0	0	0
Western Slope (Other)*	0	0	0	0	0	0	0	0	0	0
Western Planning Area Subtotal	*8*	*0*	*35*	*0*	*22*	*0*	*13*	*0*	*0*	*0*
Central Planning Area										
Main Pass and Breton Sound	1	0	0	0	0	0	0	0	0	0
Mobile	21	0	1,788	0	1,511	0	277	3	0	47
Viosca Knoll (Shelf)	14	0	300	0	259	0	41	5	0	17
West Cameron and Sabine Pass	1	0	8	0	8	0	0	0	0	0
Central Slope (Other)**	0	0	0	0	0	0	0	0	0	0
Central Planning Area Subtotal	*37*	*0*	*2,096*	*0*	*1,778*	*0*	*318*	*8*	*0*	*64*
*Eastern Planning Area Subtotal***	*0*	*0*	*0*	*0*	*0*	*0*	*0*	*1*	*0*	*491*
GOM Total	**45**	**0**	**2,131**	**0**	**1,800**	**0**	**331**	**9**	**0**	**555**

*Western Slope (Other) includes Corpus Christi, Keathley Canyon, and Port Isabel.
**Central Slope (Other) includes Lund and Walker Ridge.
***Eastern Planning Area includes DeSoto Canyon, Destin Dome, Lloyd Ridge, and others.

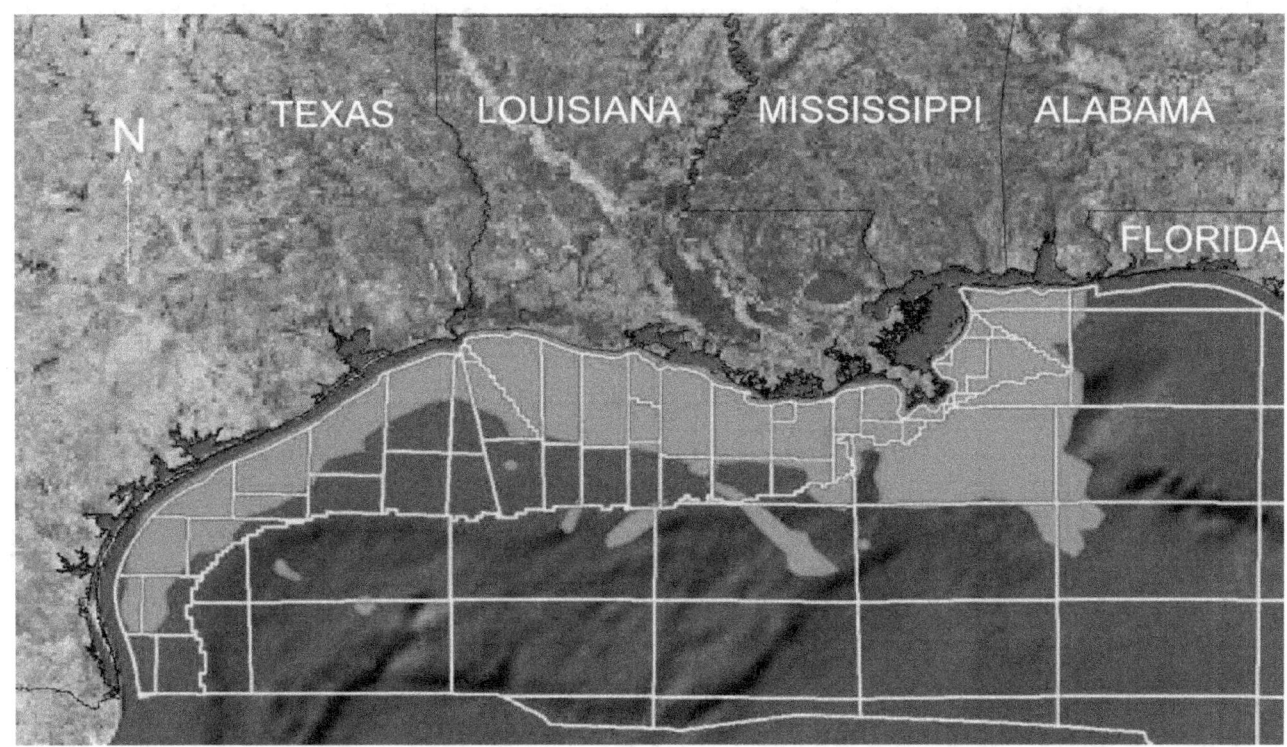

Figure 12. Miocene reserves trend.

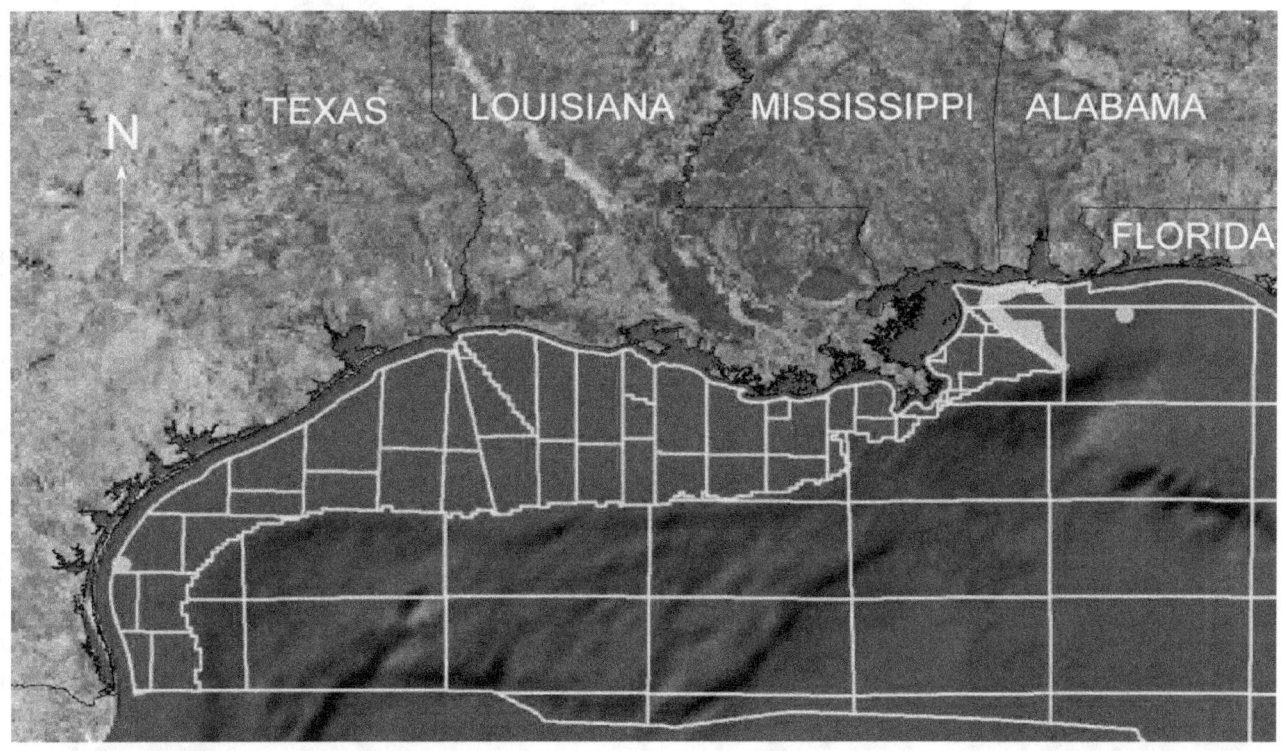

Figure 13. Pre-Miocene reserves trend.

Table 3e. Estimated oil and gas reserves for reservoirs that Span Ages in 7 proved and 13 unproved fields by area, Gulf of Mexico, Outer Continental Shelf, December 31, 2006.

(Reserves: oil expressed in millions of barrels at 60 ºF and 1 atmosphere, gas in billions of cubic feet at 60 ºF and 15.025 psia)

Area	Number of proved reservoirs	Proved reserves		Cumulative production through 2006		Remaining proved reserves		Number of unproved reservoirs	Unproved reserves	
		Oil	Gas	Oil	Gas	Oil	Gas		Oil	Gas
Western Planning Area										
Alaminos Canyon	8	272	328	0	0	272	328	10	130	270
Western Slope (Other)*	0	0	0	0	0	0	0	4	1,349	300
Western Planning Area Subtotal	*8*	*272*	*328*	*0*	*0*	*272*	*328*	*14*	*1,479*	*570*
Central Planning Area										
Atwater Valley	19	51	48	0	0	51	48	13	77	228
Green Canyon	26	1,280	759	31	14	1,249	745	34	793	373
Central Slope (Other)**	0	0	0	0	0	0	0	10	850	159
Central Planning Area Subtotal	*45*	*1,331*	*807*	*31*	*14*	*1,300*	*793*	*57*	*1,720*	*760*
*Eastern Planning Area Subtotal****	*0*	*0*	*0*	*0*	*0*	*0*	*0*	*0*	*0*	*0*
GOM Total	*53*	*1,603*	*1,135*	*31*	*14*	*1,572*	*1,121*	*71*	*3,199*	*1,330*

*Western Slope (Other) includes Corpus Christi, Keathley Canyon, and Port Isabel.
**Central Slope (Other) includes Lund and Walker Ridge.
***Eastern Planning Area includes DeSoto Canyon, Destin Dome, Lloyd Ridge, and others.

Figure 14 shows the percentages of reserves and production data by geologic age. This figure matches the chronostratigraphy by the MMS in the abbreviated Gulf of Mexico biostratigraphic chart presented in **Figure 9**. This figure exhibits that Miocene is the predominant reserves trend in the Gulf of Mexico, with the largest percentage of proved reserves, cumulative production, and remaining proved reserves.

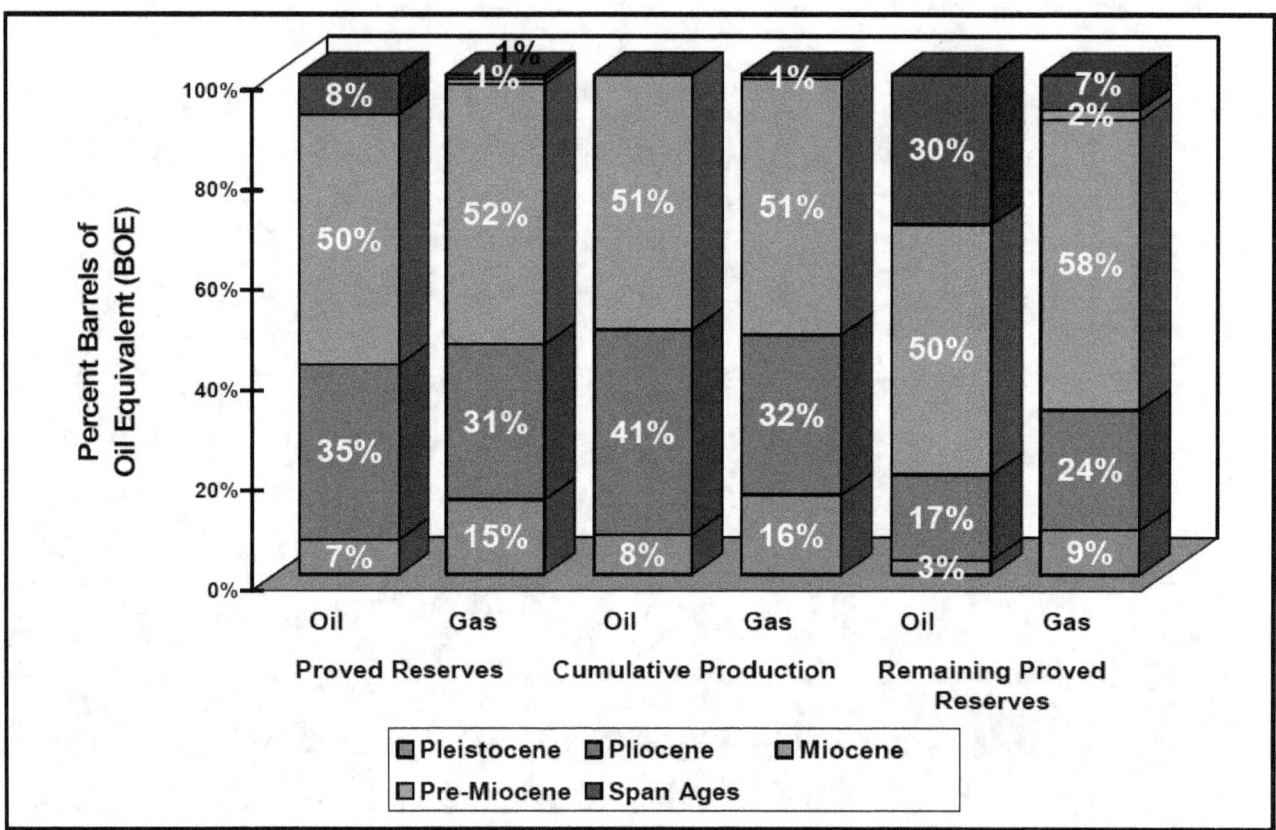

Figure 14. Distribution of reserves and production data by geologic age.

18

Historical Exploration and Discovery Pattern and Trends

In large part, the following section was taken from *An Exploration and Discovery Model: a Historic Perspective - Gulf of Mexico Outer Continental Shelf* by Gary Lore (1994). The information presented has been updated to reflect the current database.

It is informative to review the historic exploration and development activities that resulted in the world-class hydrocarbon-producing basin that is the Gulf of Mexico. Each of the decades of activity will be examined by reviewing the status of exploration and development activity and the number of fields and quantities of proved reserves discovered during each decade. The discovery year is defined as the year in which the first well encountering significant hydrocarbons reached total depth. This date may differ from the year in which the field discovery was announced.

Figures 15-20 depict locations of proved fields by decade with bar heights proportional to total proved reserves in barrels of oil equivalent (BOE). **Figure 15** shows the locations of the proved fields discovered prior to December 31, 1959. As expected, initial development was in shallower, nearshore waters concentrated mainly in the areas off central and western Louisiana. This primarily reflected the gradual extension of existing inland drilling and development technologies into the open-water marine environments, and the infancy of marine seismic acquisition activities. Early exploratory drilling in very shallow water on the shelf utilized barges and platforms. The mid-1950's witnessed the introduction of submersible and jack-up drilling rigs. During this period, 283 exploratory wells were drilled, culminating in the discovery of 68 proved fields. It was also during this period that 5 of the top 10 fields in the Gulf of Mexico, based on proved reserves, were discovered, the largest being West Delta 30.

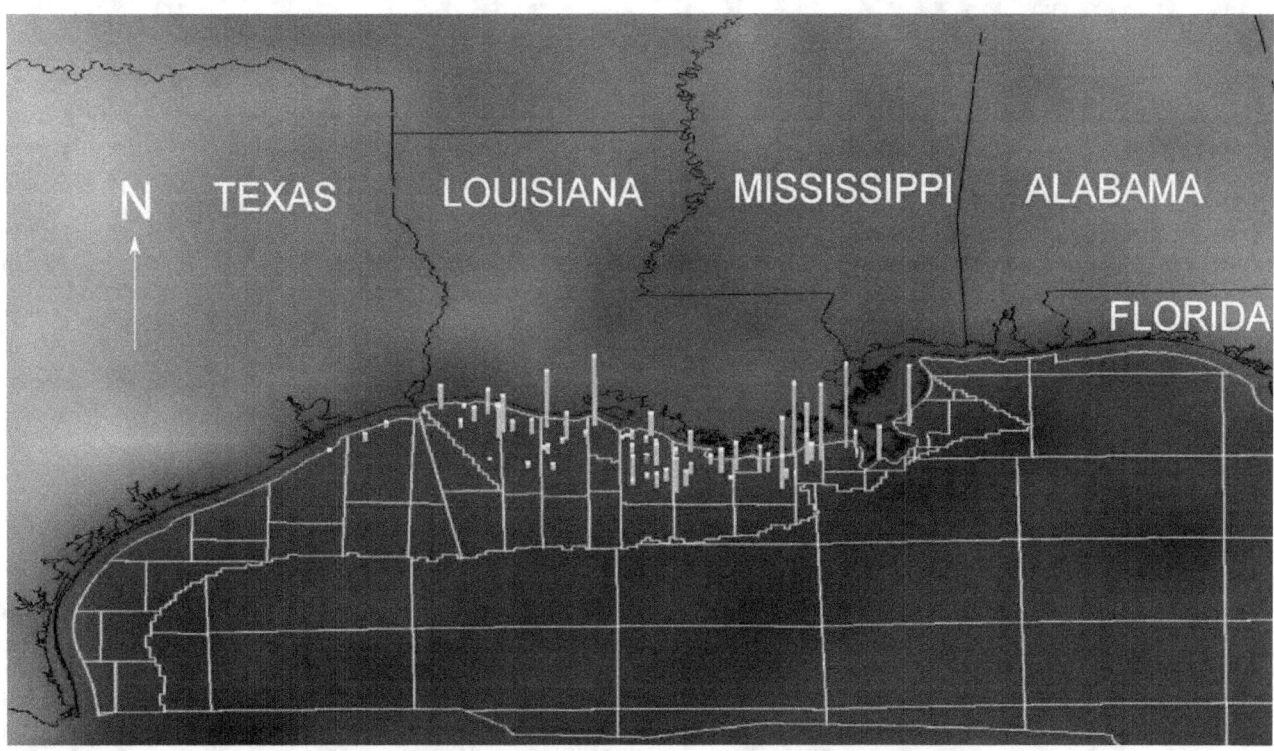

Figure 15. Location of proved fields discovered 1947-1959, Gulf of Mexico OCS.

Figure 16 shows the location of the proved fields discovered in the 1960's. These discoveries were still concentrated offshore central and western Louisiana. Though still confined to the shelf (650 ft or less), field discoveries advanced seaward into deeper waters. During this decade, 2,149 exploratory wells were drilled and 149 proved fields discovered. The thirteenth largest proved field in the Gulf of Mexico, Ship Shoal 208, was discovered in the sixties.

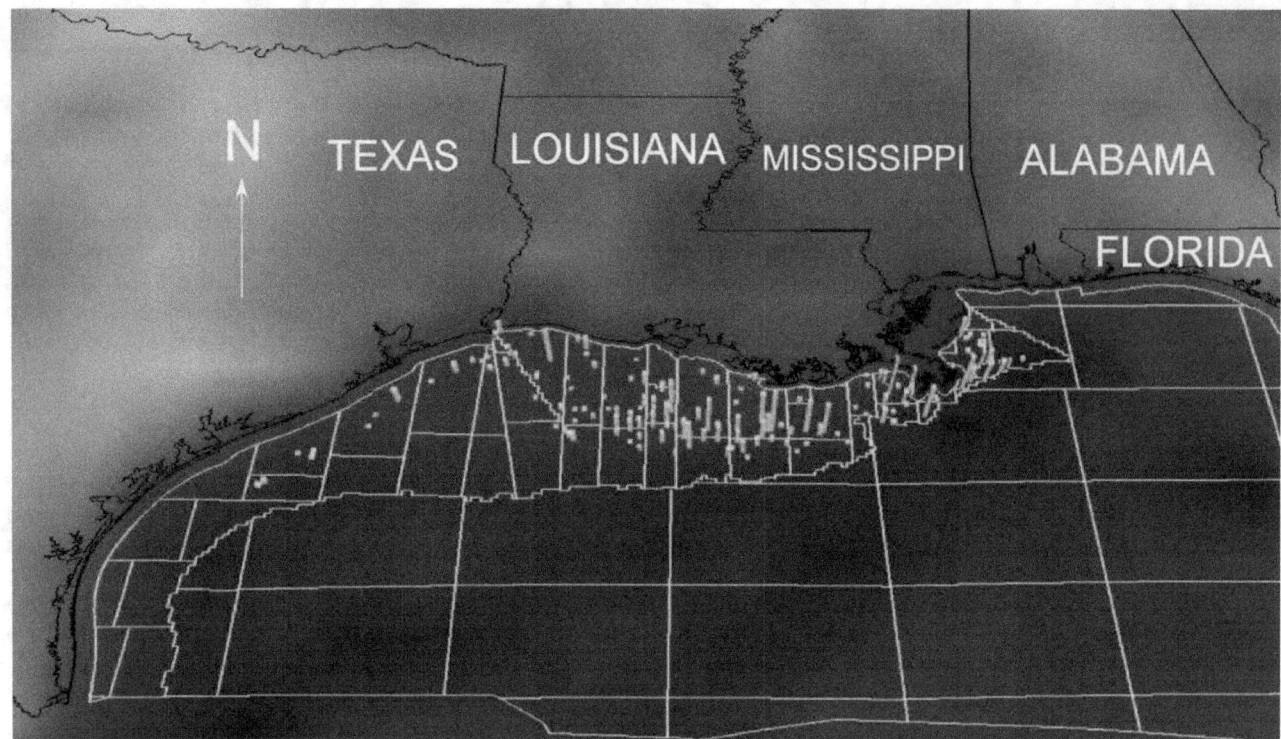

Figure 16. Location of proved fields discovered 1960-1969, Gulf of Mexico OCS.

Figure 17 shows the location of the proved fields discovered in the 1970's. This period reflects continued drilling and development on the shelf, with an increase in field discoveries on the seaward portion of the shelf, predominantly of Pleistocene age. The introduction of global positioning systems, used on drillships and semi-submersible drilling rigs, further opened up deepwater exploration. Frontier drilling on the shelf-slope margin led to discoveries of new fields in what has been termed the Flexure Trend. During this decade, 3,083 exploratory wells were drilled, resulting in the discovery of 281 proved fields. The second largest field in the Gulf of Mexico, Eugene Island 330, was discovered in 246 ft of water during this decade. Another significant field discovery was Mississippi Canyon 194, the first field in over 1,000 ft of water.

During the 1980's, development activities occurred over practically the entire central and western Gulf of Mexico shelf, as well as on the upper slope, as can be seen in **Figure 18**. In addition, the first Norphlet fields and a Miocene shallow bright spot play were discovered in the eastern Central Gulf of Mexico planning area. Exploratory drilling had now reached water depths beyond 6,000 ft. In this decade, 4,429 exploration wells were drilled, resulting in the discovery of 372 proved fields (30 were discovered in water depths greater than 1,000 ft). The largest field in the Gulf of Mexico, MC807, was discovered during this time period.

For the 1990's (**Figure 19**), 4,103 exploration wells were drilled, resulting in the discovery of 222 proved fields (52 were discovered in water depths greater than 1,000 ft). The 1990's saw the refinement and reduction in cost of tension leg platform design and a much expanded use of subsea completions. Available production histories have documented high production rates for deepwater fields. The expanding use of horizontal drilling increased productivity of specific reservoirs. Computer workstation technology using three-dimensional seismic data sets allowed for reduced risk and greater geologic assurance in exploration and field development, as well as exploration of new plays, such as the subsalt play. The fourth largest field in the Gulf of Mexico, MC778, was discovered in the nineties.

From 2000 to 2006 (**Figure 20**), 2,643 exploration wells were drilled, resulting in the discovery of 137 proved fields. Nearly 29 percent of those fields were in greater than 1,000 ft of water. Reserve estimates for field discoveries during this period may have significant increases because of increased well control, reservoir management, and in-field exploration. MC776, the sixth largest field in the Gulf of Mexico, was discovered during this time period.

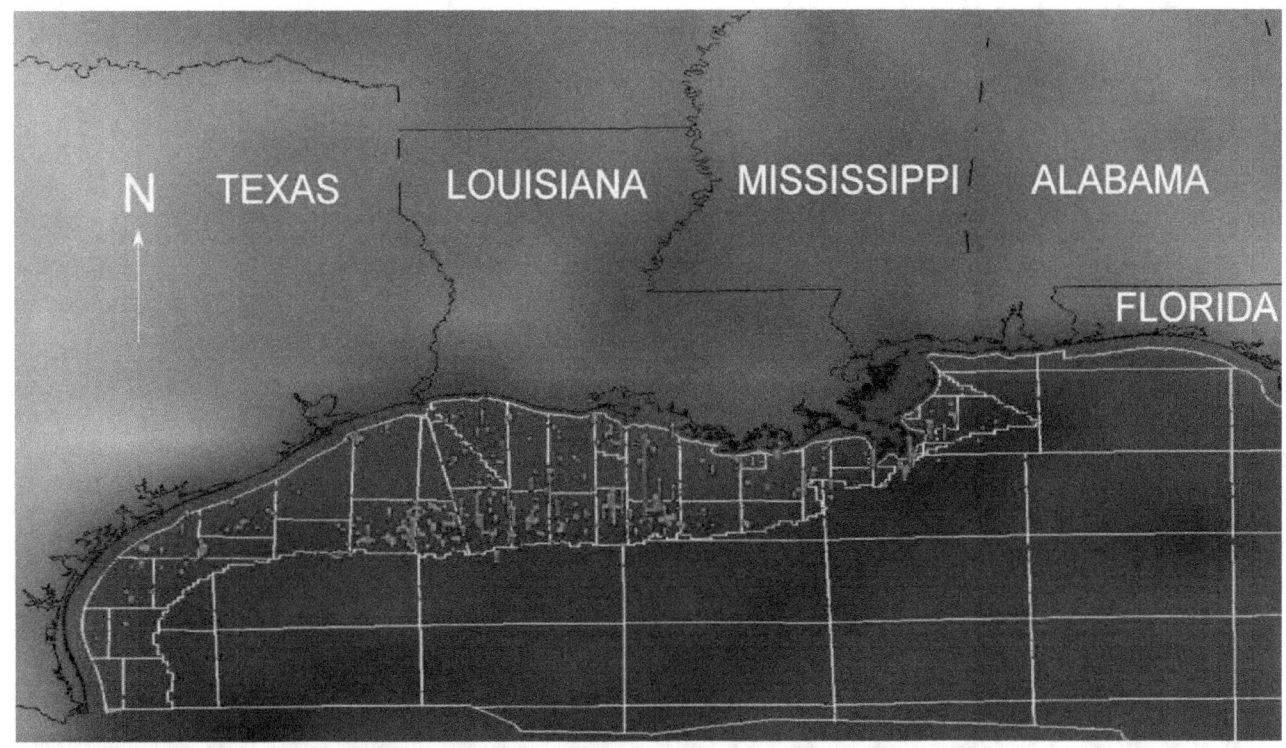

Figure 17. Location of proved fields discovered 1970-1979, Gulf of Mexico OCS.

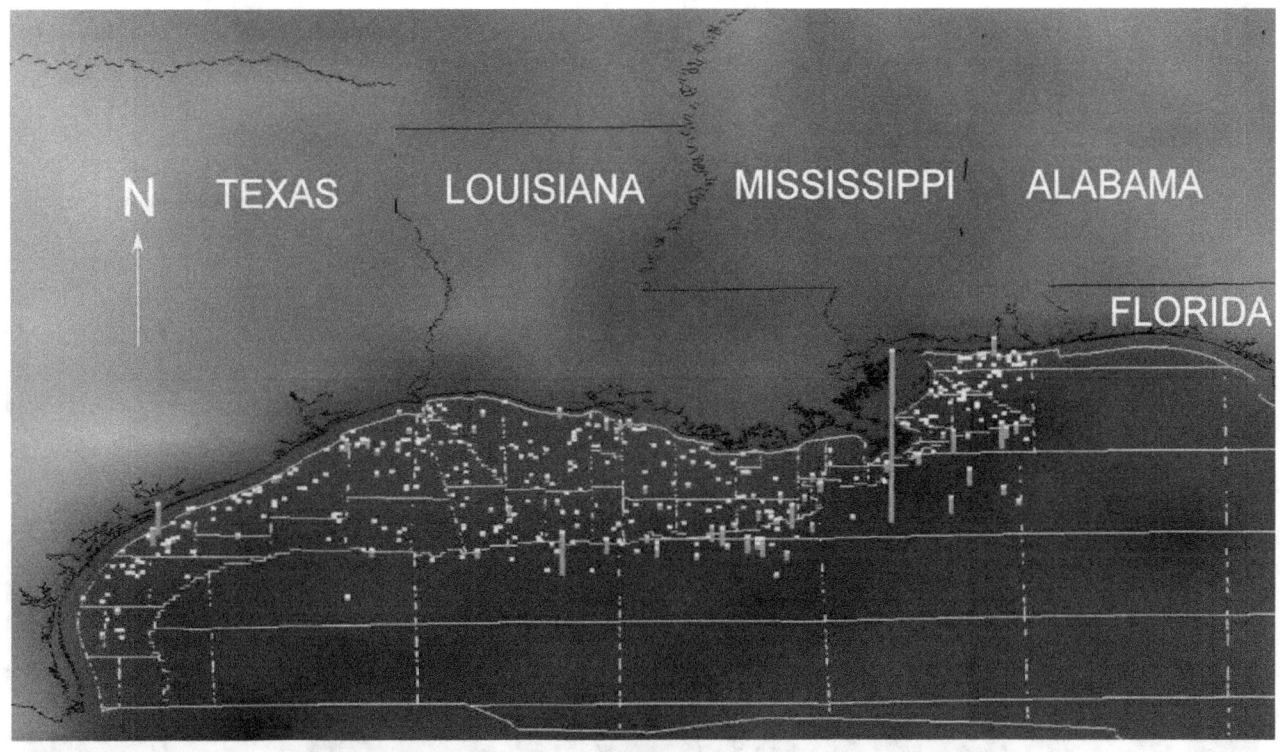

Figure 18. Location of proved fields discovered 1980-1989, Gulf of Mexico OCS.

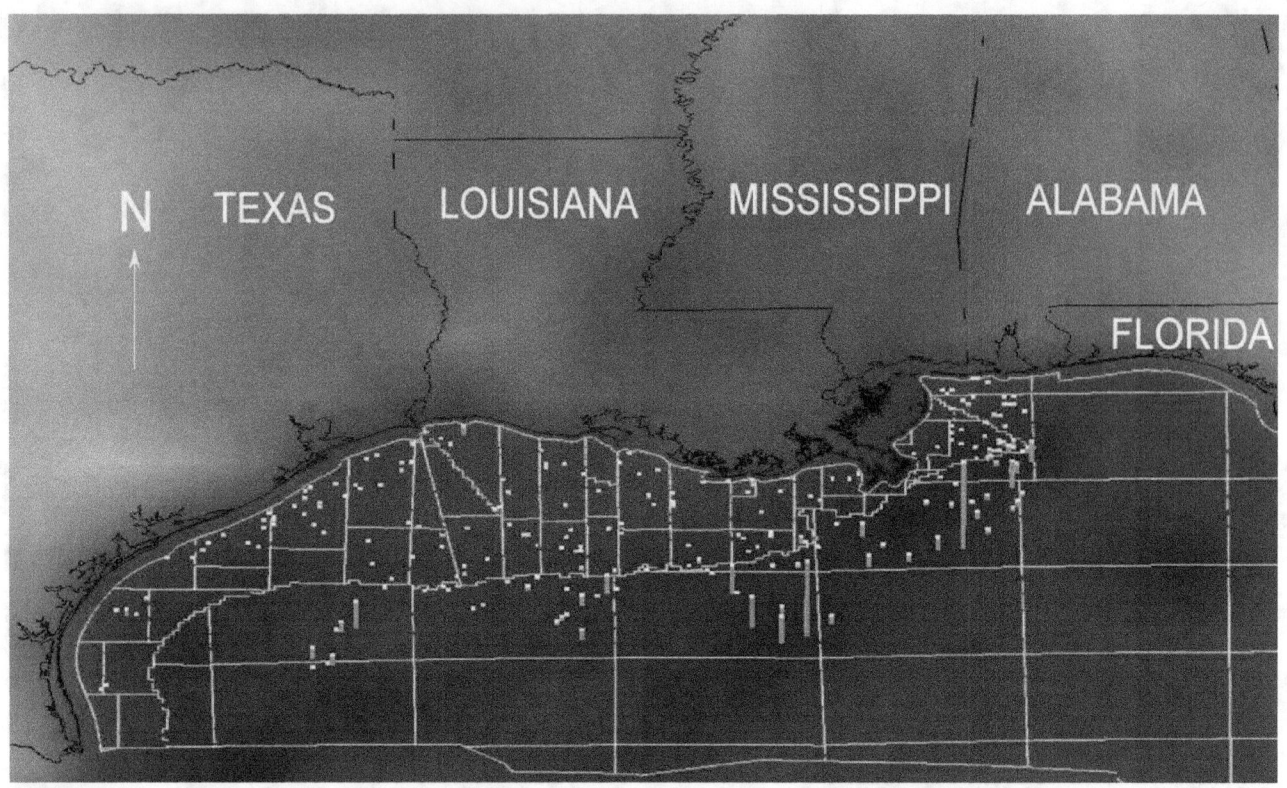

Figure 19. Location of proved fields discovered 1990-1999, Gulf of Mexico OCS.

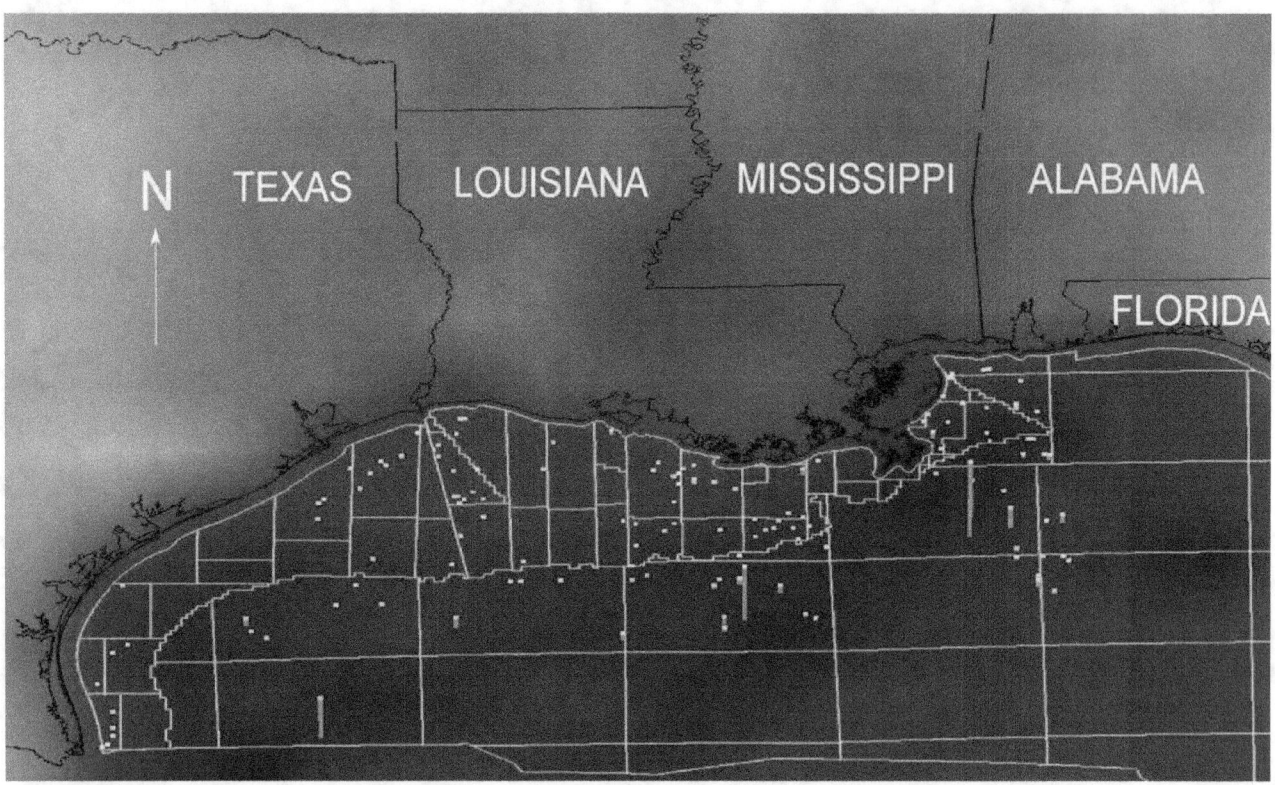

Figure 20. Location of proved fields discovered 2000-2006, Gulf of Mexico OCS.

Figure 21 shows annual field discoveries by geologic age for the 1,229 proved fields. **Figure 22** shows annual discoveries of proved reserves by geologic age for the 1,229 proved fields. These two figures show several trends over the last 50 years. From the mid-1940's through the 1960's, the largest number of fields discovered were of Miocene age and these fields contributed the largest reserves additions. This trend reflects a continuation of the nearshore operating environment. The decade of the 1970's saw a large peak in the discovery of Pleistocene and Pliocene fields and proved reserves. Technological advances in seismic data and deeper drilling accounted for the resurgence of Miocene field discoveries and reserve additions in the decade of the 1980's. This decade also saw the first Jurassic Norphlet discoveries. The decline in the number of fields discovered from 2001 to 2006 may in part be due to changes in industry exploration trends and active hurricane seasons. Large Miocene and Pliocene discoveries in the late 1990's will play a major role in future production. The MMS OCS Report MMS 2009-016, *Deepwater Gulf of Mexico 2009: Interim Report of 2008 Highlights,* available from MMS's Gulf of Mexico Region Internet Web site, provides detailed information on deepwater activities.

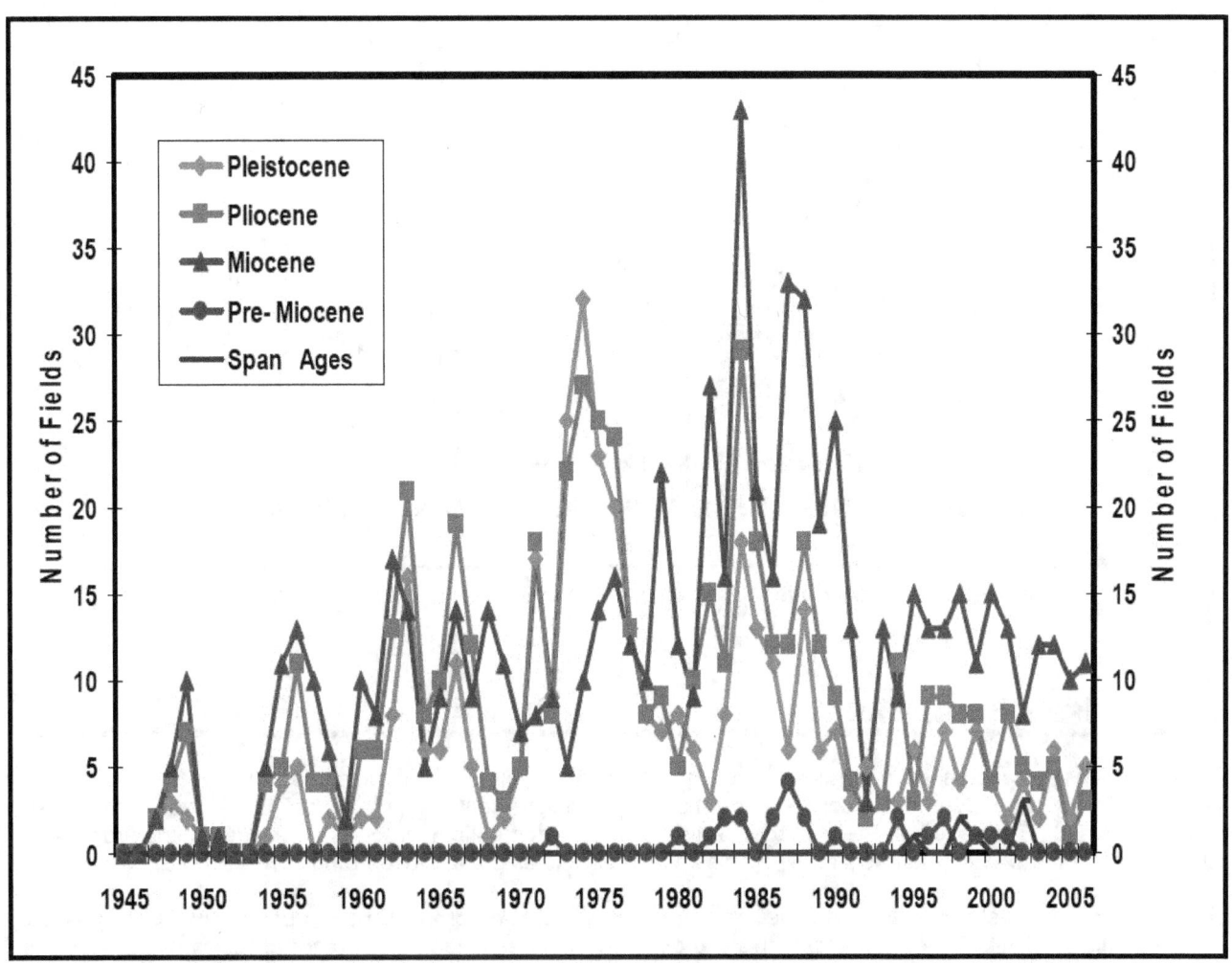

Figure 21. Annual number of field discoveries by geologic age, 1,229 proved fields.

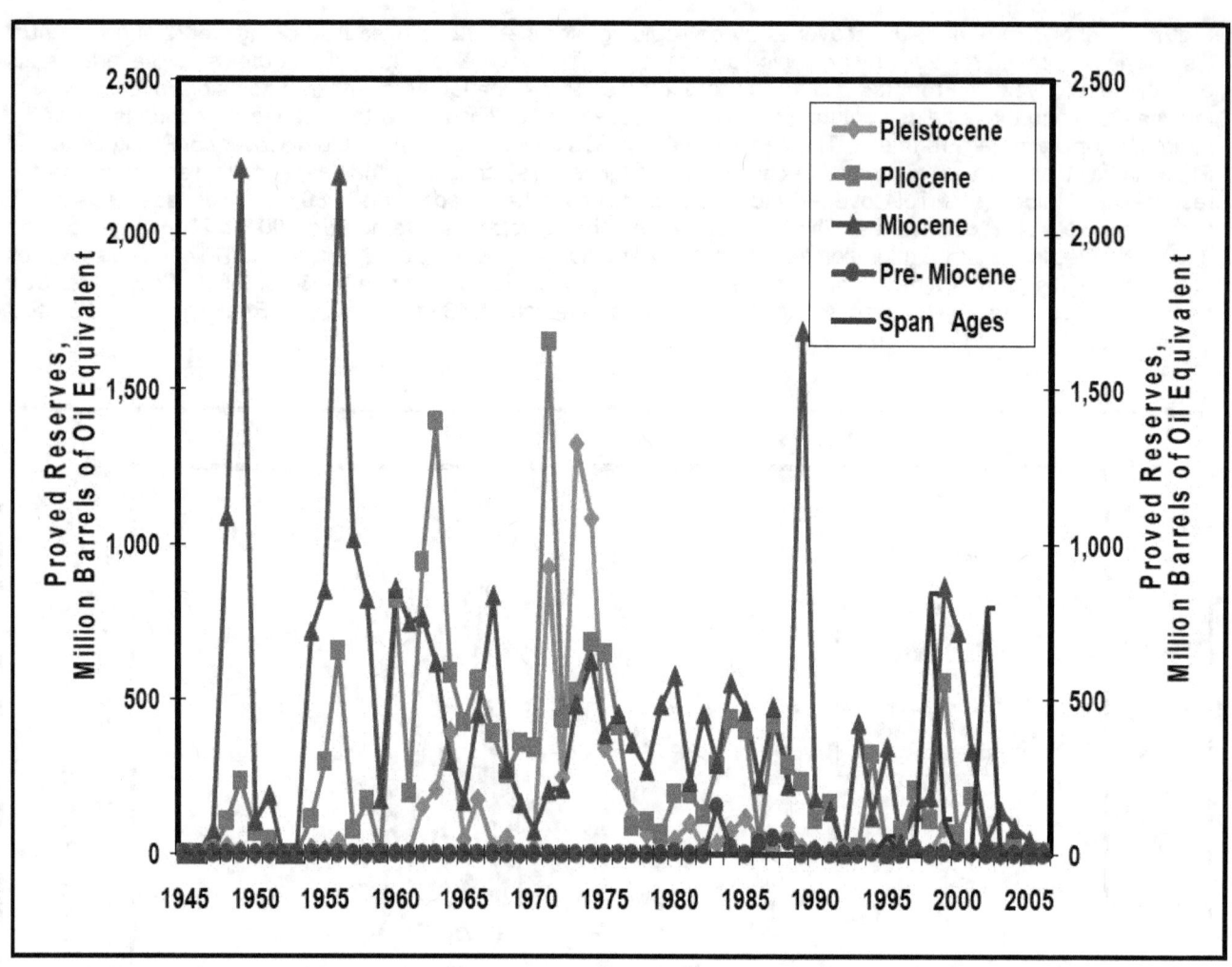

Figure 22. Annual discoveries of proved reserves by geologic age, 1,229 proved fields.

Field-Size Distribution

Reserve sizes are expressed in terms of barrels of oil equivalent (BOE). Gas reserves are converted to BOE and added to the liquid reserves for the convenience of comparison. The conversion factor of 5,620 standard cubic feet of gas equals 1 BOE is based on the average heating values of domestic hydrocarbons. A geometric progression, developed by the USGS (Attanasi, 1998), was selected for field-size distribution ranges (**Figure 23**).

In this report, fields are classified as either oil or gas; some fields do produce both products, making a field type determination difficult. Generally, fields with a gas/oil ratio (GOR) less than 9,700 standard cubic feet per stock tank barrel (SCF/STB) are classified as oil.

Class	Deposit-size range*	Class	Deposit-size range*	Class	Deposit-size range*
1	0.031 - 0.062	10	16 - 32	18	4,096 - 8,192
2	0.062 - 0.125	11	32 - 64	19	8,192 - 16,384
3	0.125 - 0.25	12	64 - 128	20	16,384 - 32,768
4	0.25 - 0.50	13	128 - 256	21	32,768 - 65,536
5	0.50 - 1.00	14	256 - 512	22	65,536 - 131,072
6	1 - 2	15	512 - 1,024	23	131,072 - 262,144
7	2 - 4	16	1,024 - 2,048	24	262,144 - 524,288
8	4 - 8	17	2,048 - 4,096	25	524,288 - 1,048,576
9	8 - 16	*Million Barrels of Oil Equivalent (MMBOE)			

Figure 23. Description of deposit-size classes.

The field-size distribution based on proved reserves for 1,229 proved fields is shown in **Figure 24(a)**. Of the 1,229 proved oil and gas fields, there are 230 proved oil fields represented in **Figure 25(a)** and 999 gas fields shown in **Figure 26(a)**. The Western Gulf of Mexico field-size distributions are displayed on **Figures 24(b)**, **25(b)**, and **26(b)**. **Figures 24(c)**, **25(c)**, and **26(c)** present the Central Gulf of Mexico field-size distributions of proved reserves including one field in the Eastern Gulf of Mexico. The field-size distribution, derived from unproved reserves for 59 unproved fields, is shown in **Figure 27(a)**. There are 34 unproved oil fields in **Figure 27(b)** and 25 unproved gas fields in **Figure 27(c)**. All unproved active fields were studied.

Analysis of the 1,229 proved oil and gas fields indicates that the Gulf of Mexico is historically a gas-prone basin. **Figure 28** presents the median (exceeded by 50%) and the mean (arithmetic average) reserves from the field-size distributions. This figure also provides information on the largest two field-size ranges from **Figures 24-27**. The GOR of the 230 proved oil fields is 2,554 SCF/STB. The GOR of the 34 unproved oil fields is 585 SCF/STB. The mean yield (condensate divided by gas) for the 999 proved gas fields is 22.9 barrels of condensate per million cubic feet (MMcf) of gas. The mean yield of the 25 unproved gas fields is 21.8 barrels of condensate per MMcf.

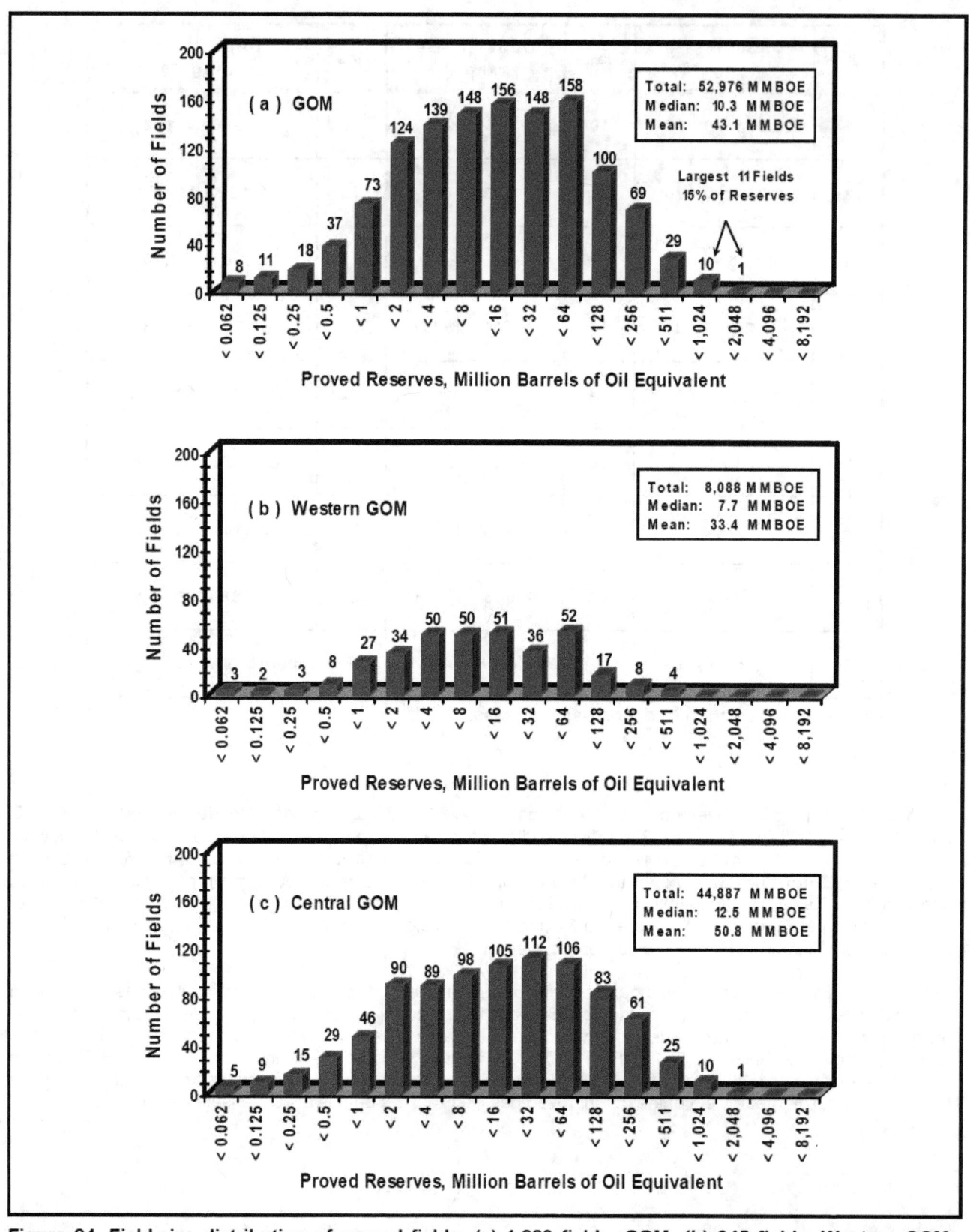

Figure 24. Field-size distribution of proved fields: (a) 1,229 fields, GOM; (b) 345 fields, Western GOM; (c) 884 fields, Central and Eastern GOM.

26

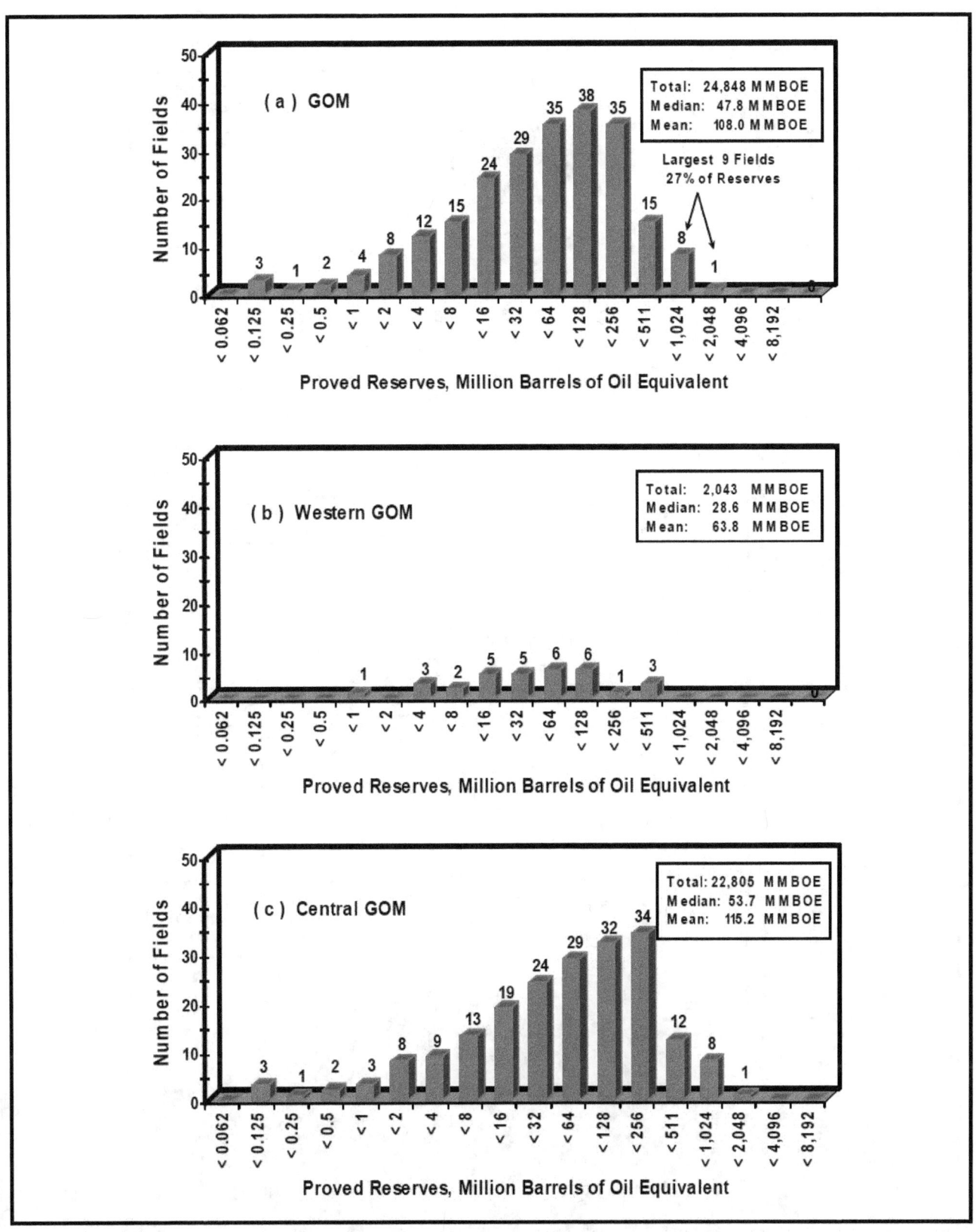

Figure 25. Field-size distribution of proved oil fields: (a) 230 fields GOM; (b) 32 fields, Western GOM; (c) 198 fields, Central and Eastern GOM.

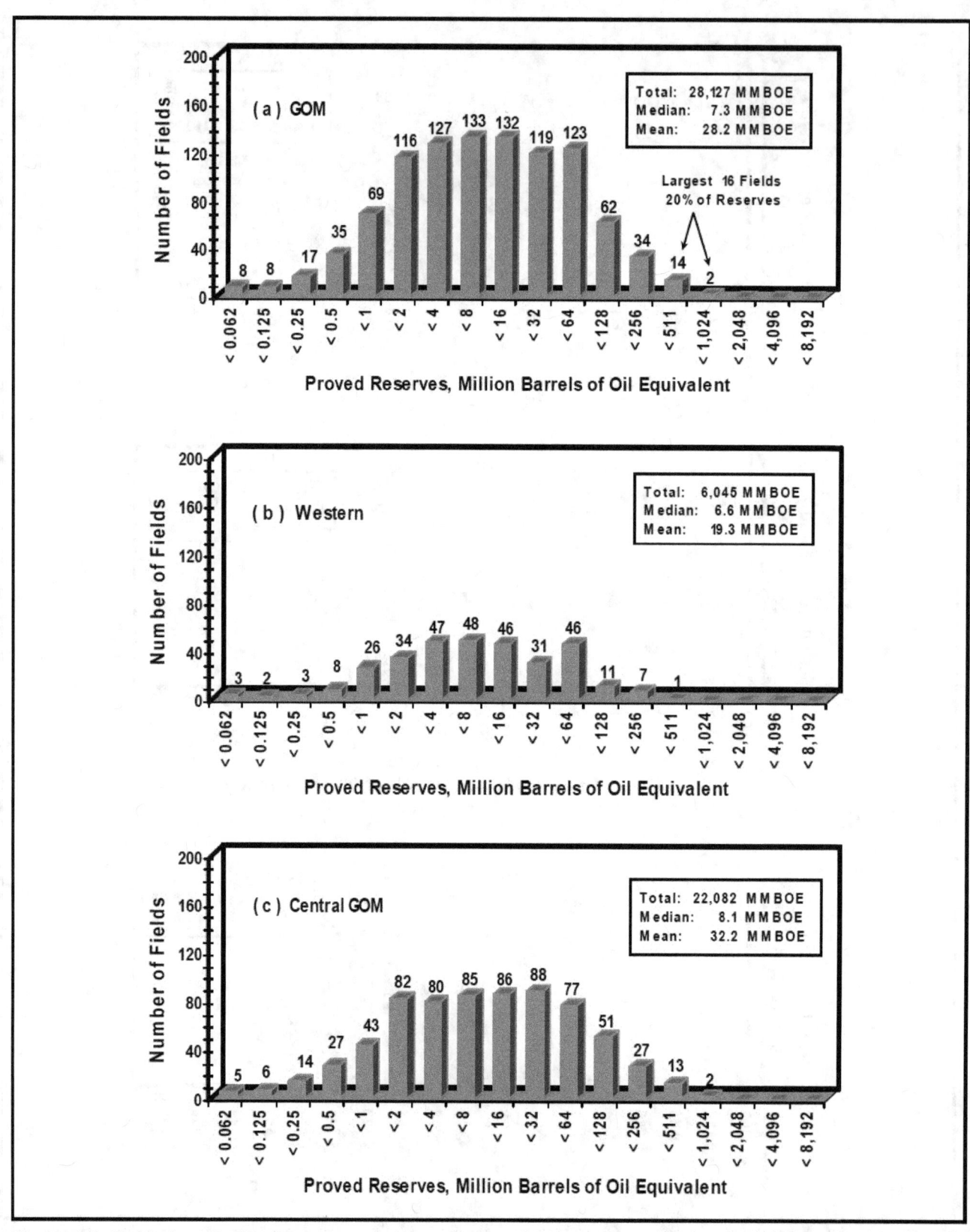

Figure 26. Field-size distribution of proved gas fields: (a) 999 fields, GOM; (b) 313 fields, Western GOM; (c) 686 fields, Central and Eastern GOM.

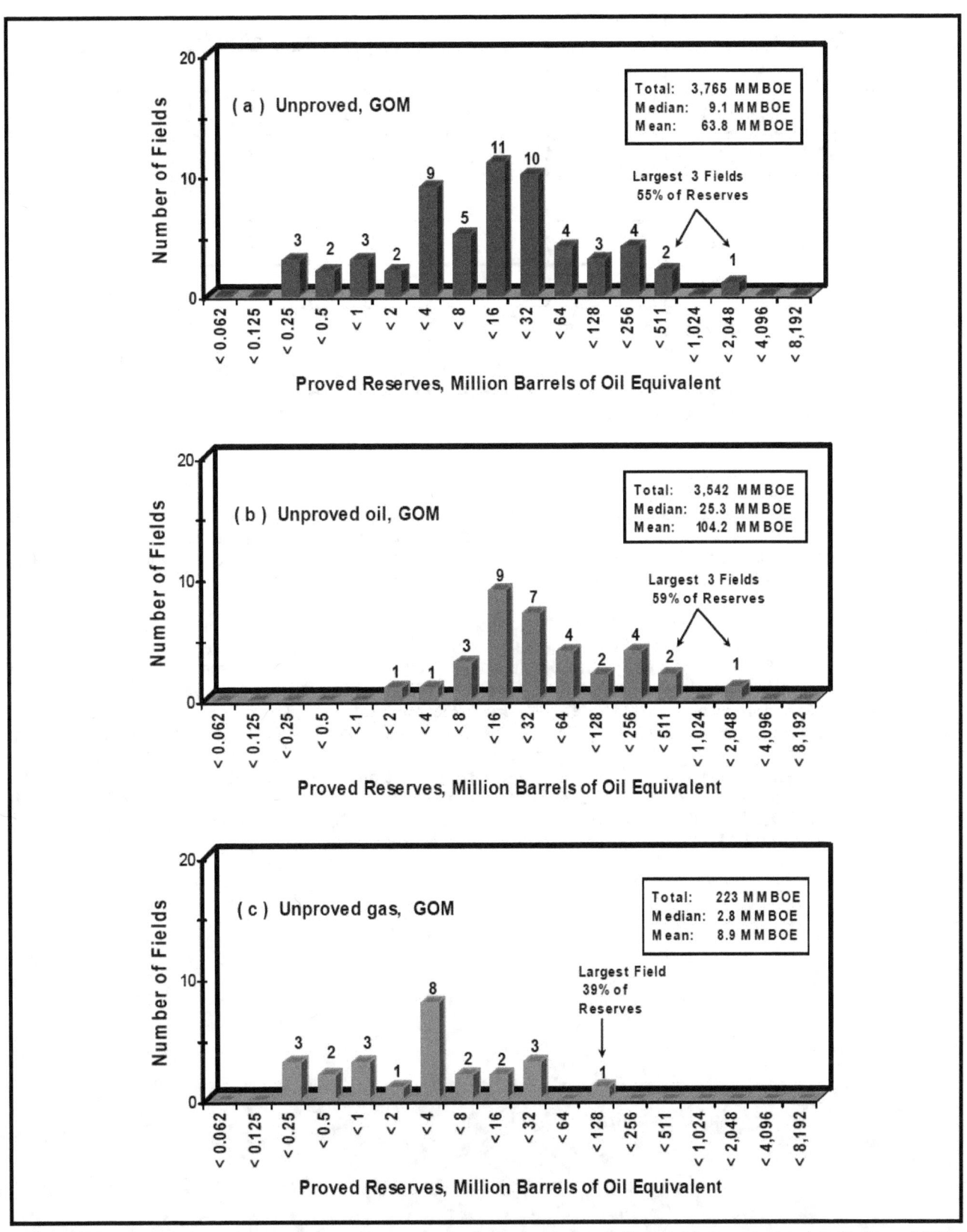

Figure 27. Field-size distribution of unproved fields: (a) 59 fields, GOM; (b) 34 oil fields, GOM; (c) 25 gas fields, GOM.

Description of Fields	Figure Number	Median*	Mean*	Largest Fields	
				Number	Reserves
1,229 Proved	Fig. 24a	10.3	43.1	11	15%
230 Proved Oil	Fig. 25a	47.8	108.8	9	27%
999 Proved Gas	Fig. 26a	7.3	28.2	16	20%
59 Unproved	Fig. 27a	9.1	63.8	3	55%
34 Unproved Oil	Fig. 27b	25.3	104.2	3	59%
25 Unproved Gas	Fig. 27c	2.8	8.9	1	39%
* Million barrels of oil equivalent (MMBOE)					

Figure 28. GOM field-size distribution.

Figure 29 shows the cumulative percent distribution of proved reserves in billion barrels of oil equivalent (BBOE), by field rank. All 1,229 proved fields in the Gulf of Mexico OCS are included in this figure. A characteristic often observed in hydrocarbon-producing basins is a rapid drop-off in size from that of largest known field to smallest. Twenty-five percent of the proved reserves are contained in the 25 largest fields. Fifty percent of the proved reserves are contained in the 84 largest fields. Ninety percent of the proved reserves are contained in the 416 largest fields.

Figure 30 shows the distribution of the number of fields and proved reserves by water depth. A field's water depth is determined by averaging the water depth of the wells drilled in the field. The water depth ranges used in this figure, 651-1,300 ft, 1,301-2,600 ft, and greater than 2,600 ft, closely approximate the 200-400 meter, 401-800 meter, and greater than 800 meter water depths used in the OCS Deepwater Royalty Relief Act of 1995 (DWRRA). Proved reserves, reported in MMBOE, are associated with the 1,229 proved fields. The 59 unproved active fields are presented to show recent activity. Fifty-six percent of the proved reserves in the Gulf of Mexico are located in less than 200 ft of water. The shelf, generally considered as less than 650 ft of water, accounts for 77 percent of the proved reserves. Development beyond the shelf, generally considered greater than 650 ft of water, reflects a sizeable amount of proved reserves associated with a few fields. The mean proved reserves per proved field in the Gulf of Mexico is 43.1 MMBOE. For water depths less than 651 ft, it is 38.4 MMBOE; for 651-1,300 ft, it is 35.3 MMBOE; for 1,301-2,600 ft, it is 45.0 MMBOE; and greater than 2,600 ft, it is 108.8 MMBOE.

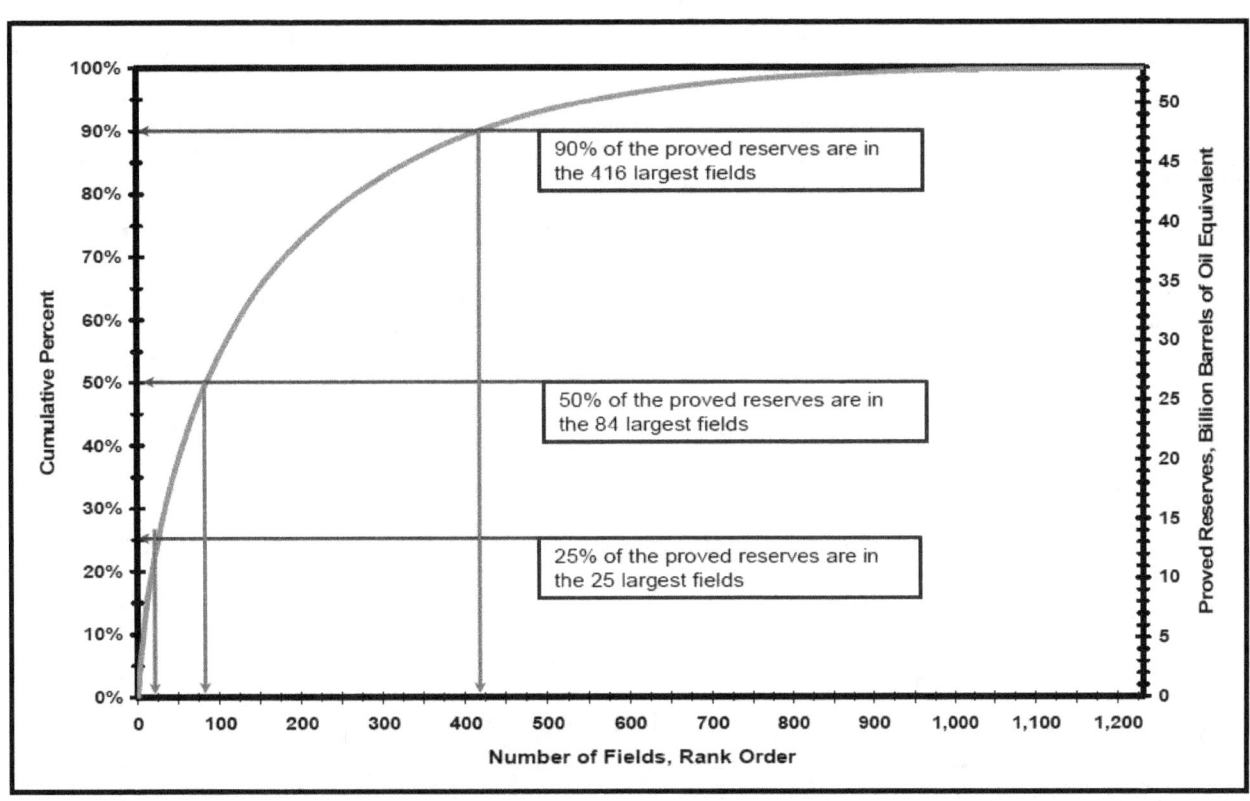

Figure 29. Cumulative percent total reserves versus rank order of field size for 1,229 proved fields.

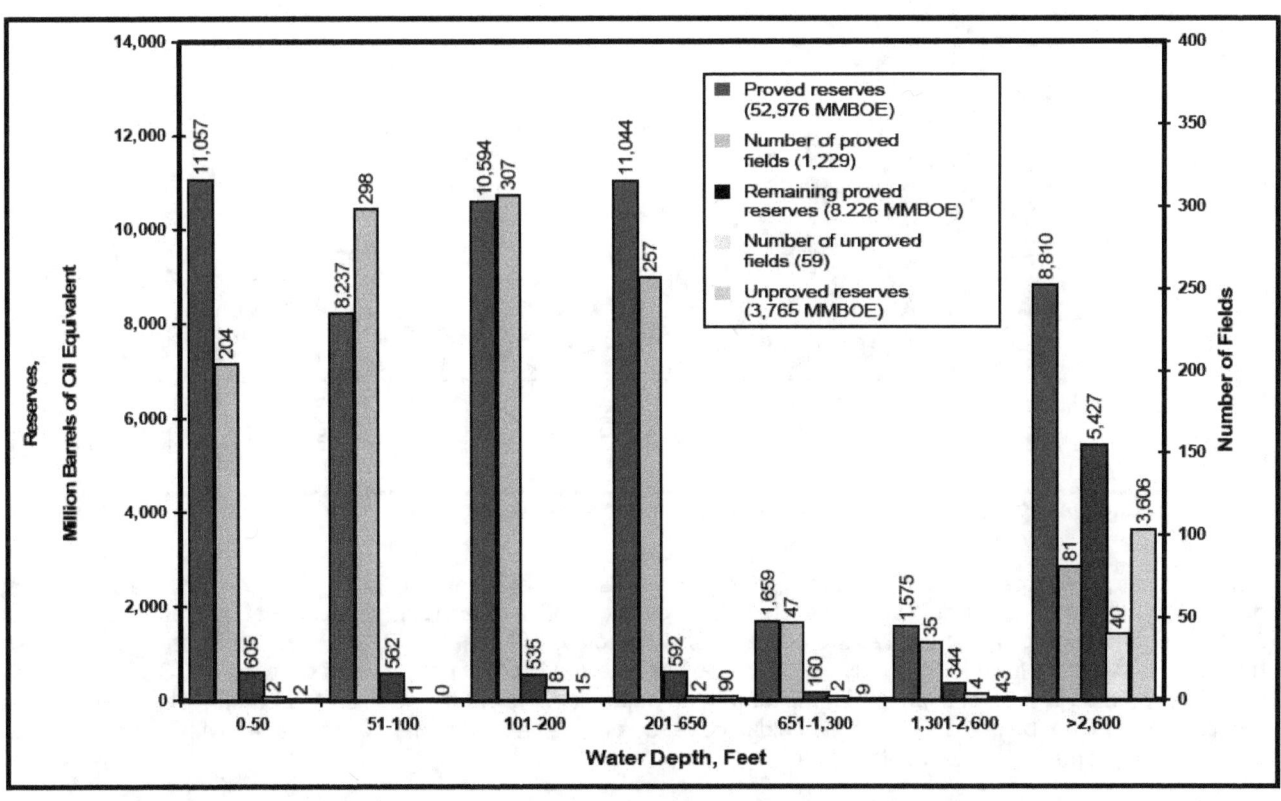

Figure 30. Field and reserves distribution by water depth. (Totals are in parentheses.)

31

Figure 31 shows the largest 20 fields ranked in order by remaining proved reserves. All 20 fields lie in water depths of greater than 1,300 ft and account for 58 percent of the remaining proved reserves in the Gulf of Mexico.

Estimates of proved reserves beyond the shelf are increasing. This trend is expected to continue in the future because of additional exploration and development. Of the 163 proved fields in water depths greater than 650 ft, 122 are producing, 20 are depleted, and 21 have yet to produce. There are 46 unproved active fields in water depths greater than 650 ft. These fields contain 3,658 MMBOE, representing 97 percent of the Gulf of Mexico total of estimated unproved reserves.

Exploration and development of the deepwater Gulf of Mexico has accelerated with technological advances, expansion of the infrastructure, and the enactment of the DWRRA. This has given industry the incentive to explore and produce deepwater resources as these activities continue to increase in importance to the Nation's energy supply.

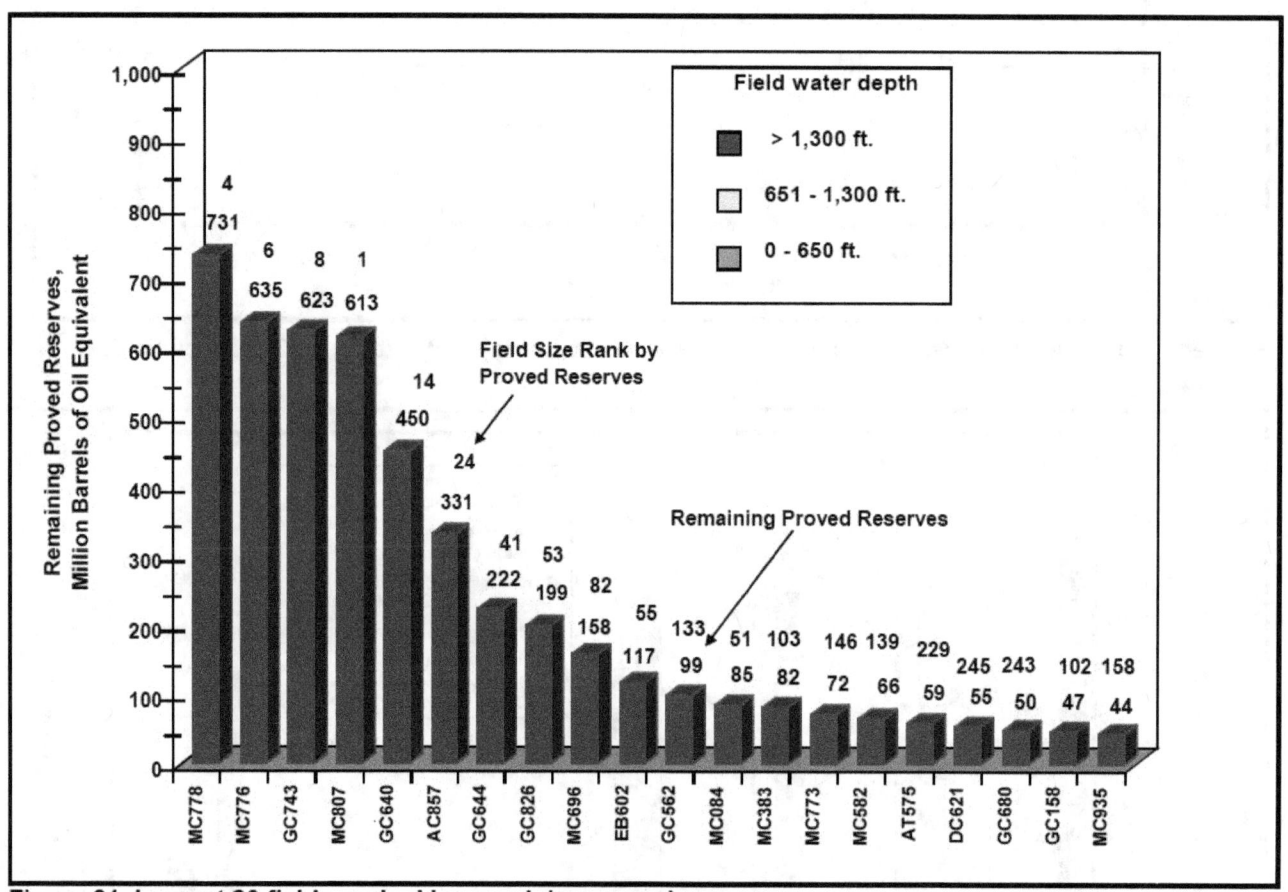

Figure 31. Largest 20 fields ranked by remaining proved reserves.

Table 4 lists the 50 largest proved fields ranked by proved reserves expressed in BOE. Rank, field name, new fields, discovery year, water depth, field classification, field type, field GOR, proved reserves, cumulative production through 2006, and remaining proved reserves are presented. A complete listing of all 1,229 proved fields, ranked by proved reserves, is available from MMS's Gulf of Mexico Region Internet Web site or by contacting the MMS at 1-800-200-GULF. New fields proved in 2006 are identified with an asterisk in the column labeled "New field." Unproved fields reserve data will not be listed. For proved fields not yet qualified, the field names are replaced with two asterisks to preserve the proprietary nature of the data.

Table 4. Gulf of Mexico proved fields by rank order, based on proved BOE reserves, top 50 fields.

(For proved fields not qualified in 2005 the names are replaced with asterisks to preserve the proprietary nature of the data.)
(Field class: PDP - Proved Developed Producing; PDN - Proved Developed Non-Producing; PU - Proved Undeveloped)
(Field type: O - Oil; G - Gas)

Rank	Field name	New field	Disc year	Water depth (feet)	Field class	Field type	Field GOR (SCF/STB)	Proved reserves			Cumulative production through 2006			Remaining proved reserves		
								Oil (MMbbl)	Gas (Bcf)	BOE (MMbbl)	Oil (MMbbl)	Gas (Bcf)	BOE (MMbbl)	Oil (MMbbl)	Gas (Bcf)	BOE (MMbbl)
1	MC807		1989	3,393	PDP	O	1,444	1,208.2	1,745 2	1,518.7	734.7	959.6	905.4	473 5	785.6	613.3
2	EI330		1971	247	PDP	O	4,222	430.9	1,819.5	754.7	420.3	1,801.4	740.9	10 6	18.1	13.8
3	WD030		1949	48	PDP	O	1,617	573.7	927.7	738.7	561.8	867.8	716.2	11 9	59.9	22.6
4	MC778		1999	6,081	PU	O	776	642.7	498.4	731.4	0.0	0.0	0.0	642 6	498.4	731.3
5	GI043		1956	140	PDP	O	4,302	377.3	1,618.9	665 3	360.8	1,537.1	634.3	16 5	81.8	31.0
6	MC776	*	2000	5,662	PU	O	1,058	534.0	565 2	634 5	0.0	0.0	0.0	534 0	565.2	634.5
7	BM002		1949	50	PDP	O	1,037	530.3	549 9	628.1	522.5	536.5	618 0	7.7	13.4	10.1
8	GC743	*	1998	6,468	PDP	O	647	558.6	361.4	623 0	0.0	0.0	0 0	558 6	361.4	622.9
9	TS000		1958	13	PDP	G	83,526	38.3	3,201.4	608 0	37.5	3,155.0	598 8	0 9	46.4	9.1
10	VR014		1956	26	PDP	G	63,983	48.2	3,082 6	596.7	47.9	3,055.7	591.6	0 3	26.8	5.1
11	MP041		1956	42	PDP	O	5,715	263.0	1,503.1	530 5	252.1	1,448.2	509.8	10 9	55.0	20.7
12	VR039		1948	38	PDP	G	81,151	31.7	2,572 6	489 5	31.2	2,542.9	483.6	0 5	29.7	5.8
13	SS208		1960	102	PDP	O	6,217	220.3	1,369 5	464 0	216.0	1,338.5	454.2	4 3	30.9	9.8
14	GC640	*	2002	4,234	PDN	O	487	414.0	201 6	449 9	0.0	0.0	0.0	414 0	201.6	449.9
15	WD073		1962	178	PDP	O	2,458	265.2	651.7	381.1	259.3	632.0	371.7	5 9	19.7	9.4
16	GB426		1987	2,860	PDP	O	3,579	229.0	819.4	374 8	211.7	757.9	346.5	17 3	61.5	28.2
17	GI016		1948	53	PDP	O	1,271	303.4	385 5	372 0	299.2	377.9	366.4	4 2	7.6	5.6
18	SP061		1967	219	PDP	O	1,930	266.9	515.1	358 5	259.5	505.1	349.4	7.4	10.0	9.1
19	ST021		1957	46	PDP	O	1,729	272.7	471.5	356 6	246.0	396.5	316.6	26.7	74 9	40.0
20	EI238		1964	147	PDP	G	16,327	91.2	1,489.5	356 3	85.8	1,423.9	339.1	5.4	65.6	17.1
21	ST172		1962	98	PDP	G	136,478	14.0	1,907 2	353 3	11.5	1,831.9	337.4	2 5	75.4	15.9
22	SP089		1969	423	PDP	O	4,448	191.1	849 9	342 3	188.3	826.4	335.3	2 8	23.5	7.0
23	WC180		1961	48	PDP	G	141,655	12.9	1,821.4	336 9	12.7	1,779.5	329.3	0 2	41.9	7.6
24	AC857	*	2002	7,900	PU	O	1,205	272.5	328 3	330 9	0.0	0.0	0 0	272 5	328.3	330.9
25	ST176		1963	126	PDP	G	14,710	89.7	1,320 0	324 6	81.5	1,171.5	290.0	8 2	148.5	34.7
26	SS169		1960	63	PDP	O	5,411	163.2	883 3	320.4	154.3	825.1	301 2	8 9	58.1	19.2
27	SM048		1961	101	PDP	G	55,963	28.6	1,601.1	313 5	27.8	1,512.7	297.0	0 8	88.4	16.5
28	MC194		1975	1,022	PDP	O	4,175	178.8	746.4	311 6	176.5	738.0	307.8	2 3	8.4	3.8
29	EC064		1957	50	PDP	G	57,810	27.4	1,586 2	309.7	26.6	1,537.9	300.3	0 8	48.4	9.4
30	EI292		1964	212	PDP	G	84,604	19.1	1,617.4	306 9	18.3	1,609.4	304.7	0 8	7.9	2.2
31	EC271		1971	171	PDP	G	18,853	70.3	1,325.8	306 2	67.5	1,309.3	300.5	2 8	16 5	5.7
32	SS176		1956	100	PDP	G	19,836	65.3	1,294 6	295 6	62.9	1,261.7	287.4	2 3	32.9	8.2
33	SP027		1954	64	PDP	O	5,219	151.7	791 6	292 5	150.0	762.3	285.7	1.7	29.3	6.9
34	WC587		1971	211	PDP	G	110,142	14.1	1,554 0	290 6	12.8	1,528.5	284 8	1 3	25.5	5.8
35	ST135		1956	130	PDP	O	3,612	171.7	620 0	282 0	165.7	579.5	268.8	6 0	40.6	13.2
36	EI296		1971	214	PDP	G	69,965	20.3	1,421 6	273 3	20.3	1,413.6	271.8	0 0	8.0	1.5
37	WC192		1954	57	PDP	G	58,762	23.8	1,399 6	272 9	22.3	1,356.8	263.7	1 5	42.8	9.1
38	WD079		1966	124	PDP	O	3,800	162.7	618 3	272.7	160.5	609.1	268.9	2 2	9.2	3.8
39	MI623		1980	83	PDP	G	98,785	14.4	1,426 2	268 2	13.3	1,335.0	250 9	1.1	91.2	17.3
40	HI573A		1973	341	PDP	O	7,700	111.2	856 2	263 5	107.6	850.1	258.9	3 6	6.1	4.6
41	GC644		1999	4,340	PDP	O	1,234	209.6	258.7	255 6	28.0	29.4	33.3	181 5	229.3	222.3
42	GI047		1955	88	PDP	O	3,583	150.1	538 0	245 8	144.2	516.2	236.1	5 9	21.7	9.8
43	SP078		1972	203	PDP	G	11,544	77.6	896 3	237.1	72.9	881.3	229.8	4.7	15.0	7.4
44	SM023		1960	82	PDP	G	38,903	29.7	1,155.4	235 3	29.5	1,143.8	233.0	0 2	11.7	2.3
45	SM130		1973	214	PDP	O	1,341	187.4	251 3	232.1	182.8	246.0	226 6	4 5	5.3	5.5
46	PL020		1951	33	PDP	O	5,810	113.7	660 3	231 2	108.1	604.8	215.7	5 5	55.5	15.4
47	GC244		1994	2,762	PDP	O	2,005	170.3	341.5	231 0	160.0	318.8	216.7	10 3	22.7	14.3
48	VR076		1949	31	PDP	G	140,837	8.7	1,231 9	228 0	7.4	1,168.8	215.4	1.4	63.1	12.6
49	SM066		1963	124	PDP	G	255,946	4.9	1,250 3	227.4	4.8	1,218.0	221 5	0.1	32.3	5.9
50	VK956		1985	3,254	PDP	O	9,042	87.1	787 3	227 2	80.2	710.8	206.7	6 9	76.5	20.5

Reservoir-Size Distribution

The size distributions of the proved reservoirs are shown in **Figures 32**, **33**, and **34**. The size ranges are based on proved reserves and are presented on a geometrically progressing, horizontal scale. These sizes correspond with the USGS deposit-size ranges shown in Figure 23 with a modification to reflect small reservoirs in a finer distribution. For **Figures 33** and **34**, the proved reserves are presented in MMbbl and Bcf, respectively. The number of reservoirs in each size grouping, shown as percentages of the total, is presented on a linear vertical scale. For the combination reservoirs (saturated oil rims with associated gas caps), shown in **Figure 32**, gas is converted to BOE and added to the liquid reserves. Proved uneconomic reservoirs are excluded from these distributions, but are included in the **Table 3** series.

Figure 32 shows the reservoir-size distribution, on the basis of proved BOE, for 2,235 proved combination reservoirs. The median is 0.9 MMBOE and the mean is 2.9 MMBOE. The GOR for the oil portion of the reservoirs is 1,163 SCF/STB, and the yield for the gas cap is 22.1 barrels of condensate per MMcf of gas.

Figure 33 shows the reservoir-size distribution, on the basis of proved oil, for 8,014 proved undersaturated oil reservoirs. The median is 0.3 MMbbl, the mean is 1.8 MMbbl, and the GOR is 1,220 SCF/STB.

Figure 34 shows the reservoir-size distribution, on the basis of proved gas, for 17,473 gas reservoirs. The median is 2.2 billion cubic feet (Bcf) of gas, the mean is 8.6 Bcf, and the yield is 12.1 barrels of condensate per MMcf of gas.

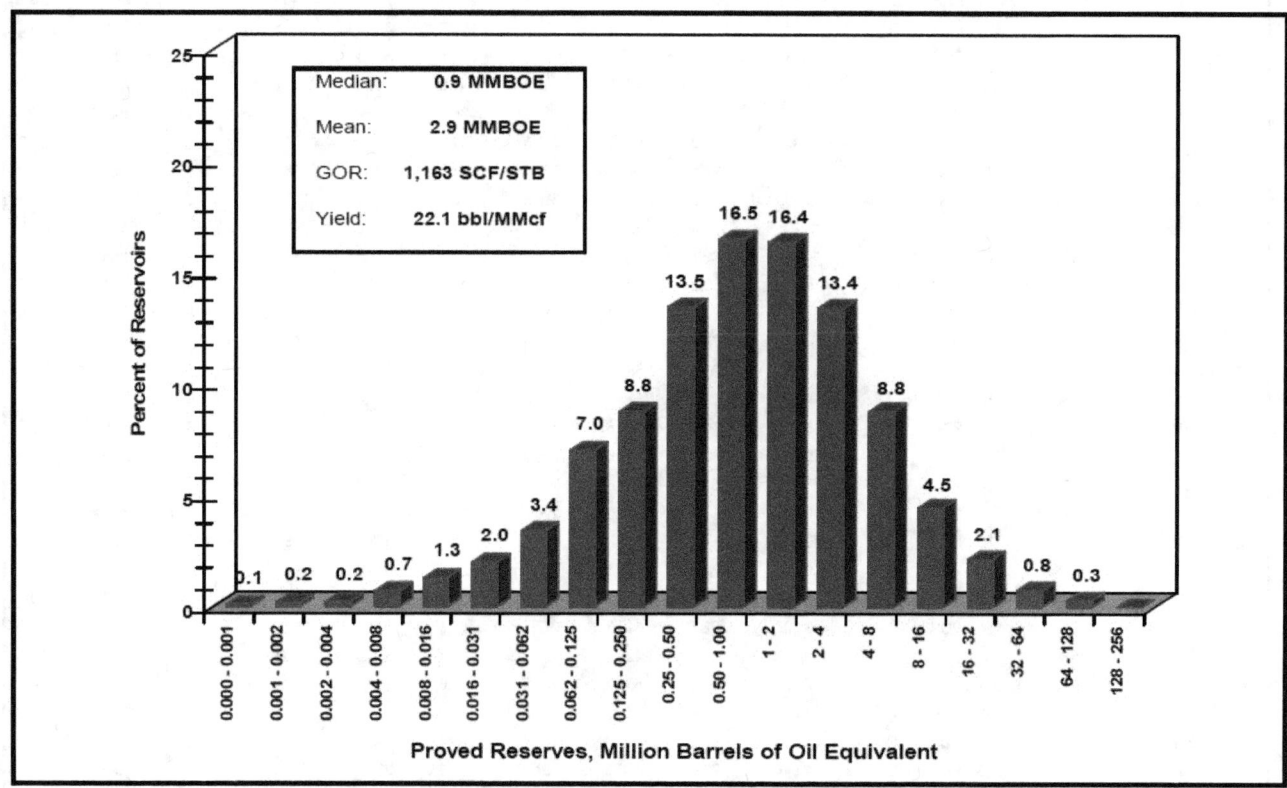

Figure 32. Reservoir-size distribution, 2,235 proved combination reservoirs.

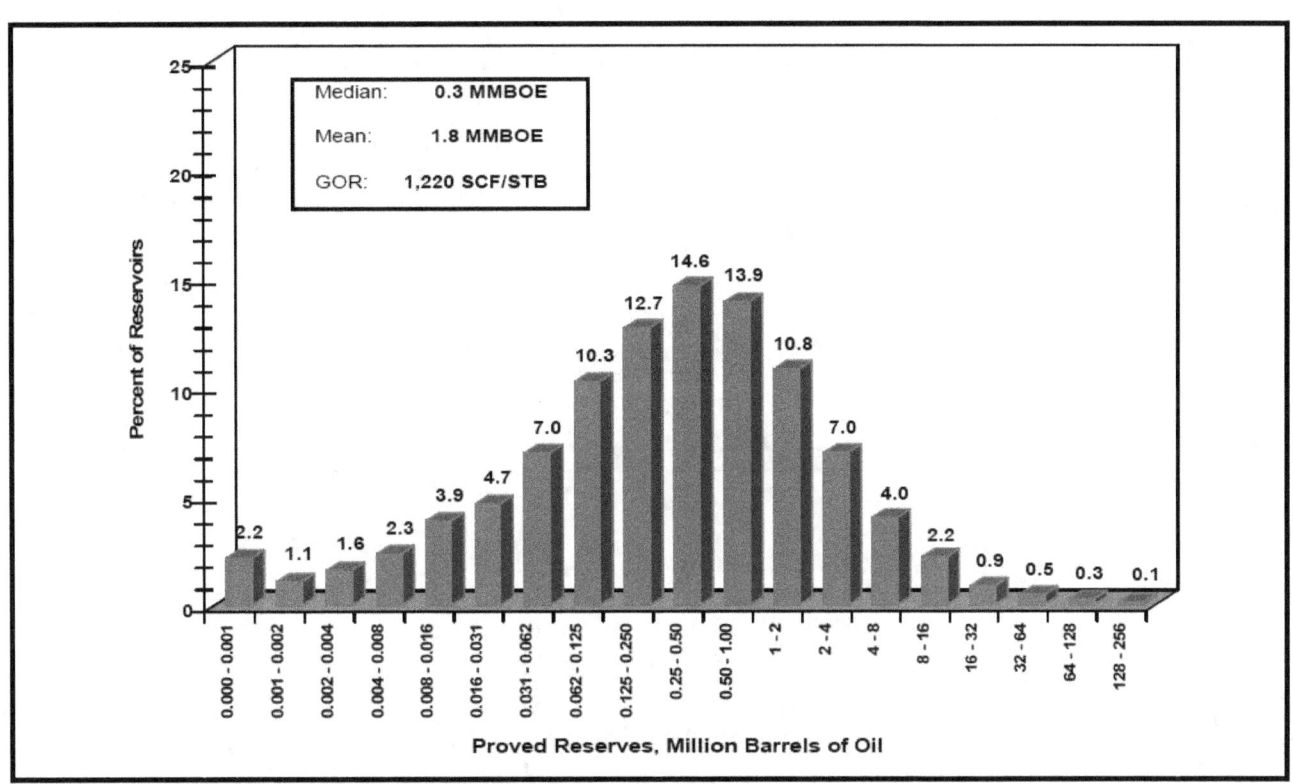

Figure 33. Reservoir-size distribution, 8,014 proved oil reservoirs.

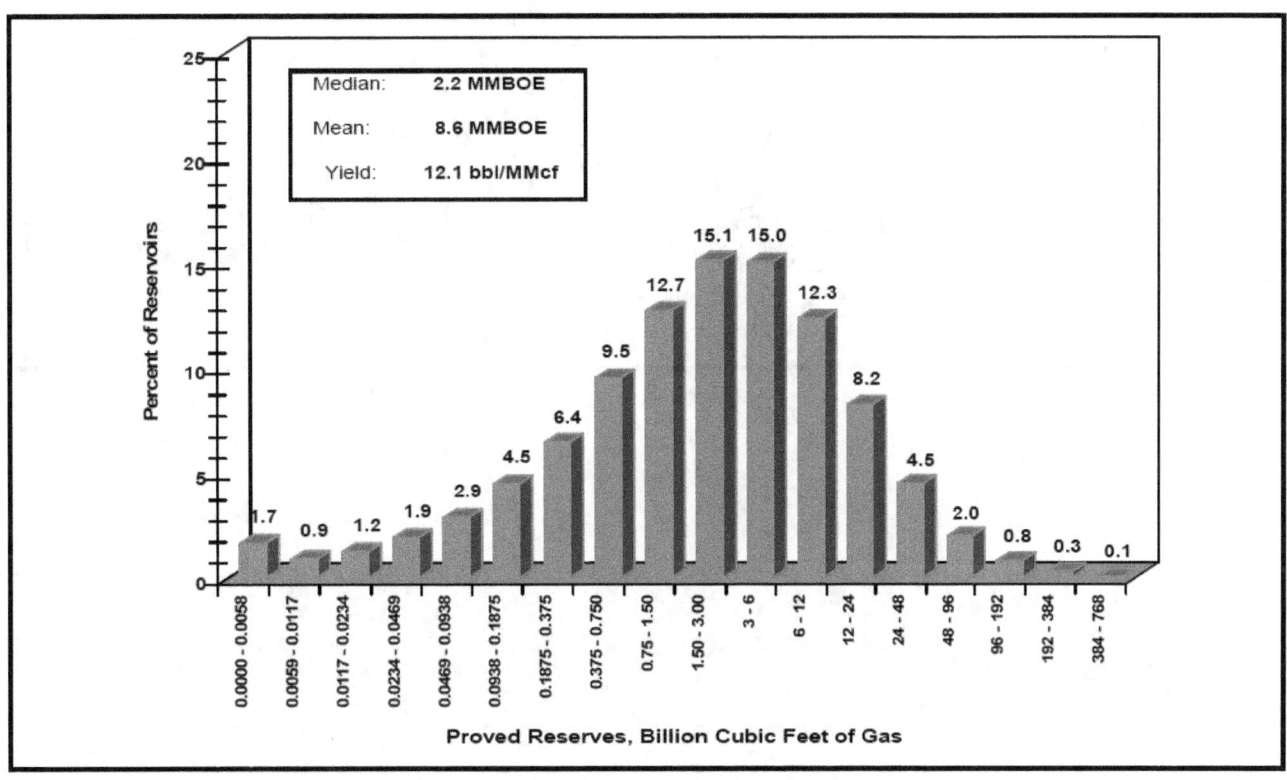

Figure 34. Reservoir-size distribution, 17,473 proved gas reservoirs.

Production Rates and Discovery Trends

The mean daily production in the Gulf of Mexico OCS during 2006 was 1.06 MMbbl of crude oil, 0.22 MMbbl of gas condensate, 1.76 Bcf of casinghead gas, and 6.25 Bcf of gas-well gas. The mean GOR of oil wells was 1,656 SCF/STB, and the mean yield from gas wells was 35.81 barrels of condensate per MMcf of gas. Monthly production plots and data by field are also available from MMS's Gulf of Mexico Region Internet Web site or can be obtained on CD-ROM by contacting the MMS at 1-800-200-GULF.

Figures 35 and **36** show the frequency distribution of monthly production for completions active during 2006. Since the number of completions within a given range changes from month to month, the completion numbers presented are means of the 2006 monthly completion totals for each production range. Completions off production for more than two days a month are not counted as continuously producing completions.

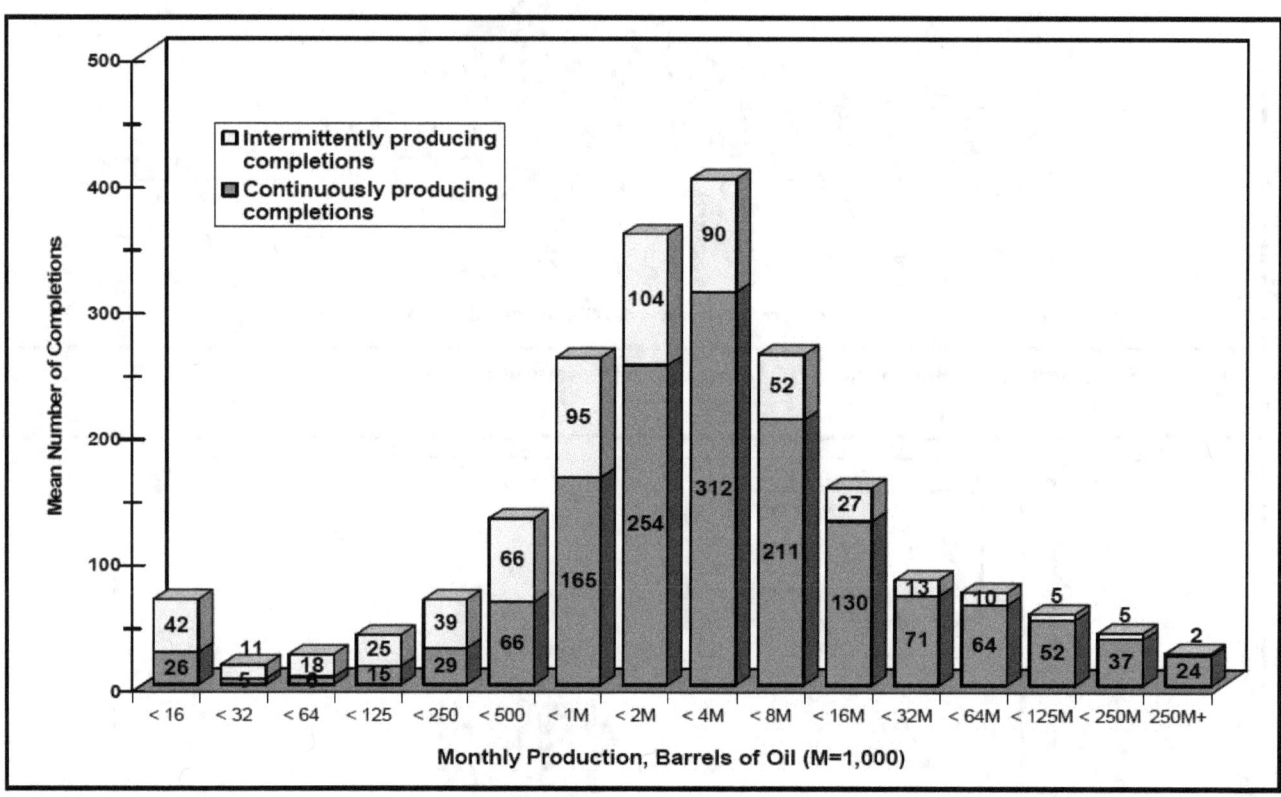

Figure 35. Monthly distribution of oil production, 2,071 completions (1,467 continuously producing completions).

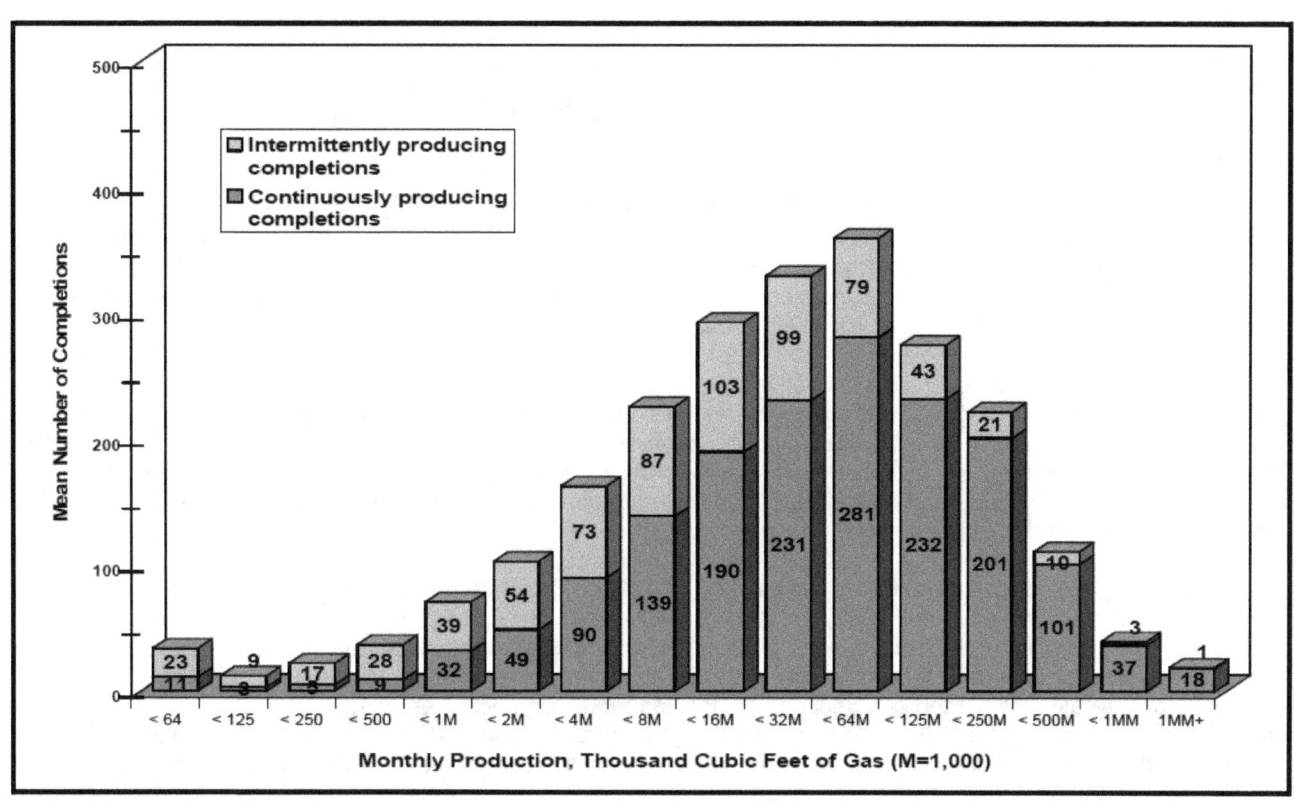

Figure 36. Monthly distribution of gas production, 2,318 completions (1,629 continuously producing completions).

Figure 37 summarizes the data from monthly distributions of oil and gas production rates. The highest reported monthly oil production volume was from a Miocene reservoir with a subsea depth of 12,300 ft, during the month of January. The highest reported monthly gas production volume was from a Miocene reservoir with a subsea depth of 15,395 ft, during the month of January. The mean number of oil completions producing more than 1,000 bbl per day was 204, and the mean number of gas completions producing more than 10 MMcf per day was 114.

2006	Oil	Gas
Mean Number of Producing Completions	2,071 (204 > 1,000 bbls per day)	2,318 (114 > 10MMcf per day)
Mean Number of Continuously Producing Completions	1,467	1,629
Highest Monthly Mean Number of Producing Completions	2,333 (December)	2,314 (January)
Lowest Monthly Mean Number of Producing Completions	1,662 (January)	38,990 (January)
Mean Production Volume / Mean Producing Rate	15,669 bbl (586 bbl per day)	81.7 MMcf (3.1 MMcf per day)
Median Production Volume / Median Producing Rate	2,257 bbl (83 bbl per day)	24.5 MMcf (1.3 MMcf per day)
Highest Production Volume / Highest Producing Rate	847,083 bbl (27,325 bbl per day)	4,287 MMcf (138.3 MMcf per day)
Highest Producing Month	(January)	(January)
Highest Production Volume Trend	(MIOCENE)	(MIOCENE)
Highest Production Volume Subsea Depth	(12,300 feet)	(15,395 feet)

Figure 37. Monthly completion and production data.

37

Annual production in the Gulf of Mexico OCS is shown in **Figure 38**. The oil plot includes condensate and the gas plot includes casinghead gas. From 1986 through 1990, annual oil production declined 23 percent, which coincides with low world oil prices. From 1990 through 2002, annual oil production increased 106 percent, from 275 MMbbl to 567 MMbbl, because of the addition of deepwater production. From 2002 to 2006 annual oil production decreased 17 percent to 468 MMbbl.

From 1990 through 1993, annual gas production declined 5 percent. From 1993 through 2001, annual gas production rose from 4.7 Tcf, peaking at 5.1 Tcf in 1997, a 9-percent increase. Annual gas production reached at least 5.0 Tcf per year from 1996 through 1999 and in 2001. From 2001 to 2006, annual gas production declined 43 percent to 2.9 Tcf. For further analysis of the gas production decline, see the MMS OCS Report MMS 2009-012, *Gulf of Mexico Oil and Gas Production Forecast: 2009-2018*, available from MMS's Gulf of Mexico Region Internet Web site.

Figure 39 presents proved reserves, cumulative production, and remaining proved reserves in BBOE as of December 31, 2006, summed according to field discovery year. Field depletion may be estimated by the relative positions of the cumulative production curve and the remaining proved reserves curve. For example, if the value of the remaining proved reserves is higher than the value of cumulative production for a given year, the aggregate depletion for fields discovered that year is less than 50 percent. The plot demonstrates in general that fields discovered after 1996 are less than 50 percent depleted.

Figure 40 is a plot of the number of proved gas and oil fields by discovery year. The annual number of gas fields discovered steadily increased until 1984, declined until 1992, increased over the next five years, declined until 2002 and slightly increased over the next 4 years. The number of oil fields discovered has not varied much from year to year, never exceeding 11, and averaging only about 3.7 discoveries per year. Through 1959, 35 percent of all fields discovered were oil. This percentage declined steadily as more gas fields were discovered. Only 14 percent of the fields discovered during the 1980's were oil fields. From 1990 through 2006, the oil fields discovered rose to 20 percent, reflecting recent deepwater discoveries. There was an average of one oil discovery per year since 2003.

Reasons for the 2001-2006 declines exhibited in **Figures 38-40** may be due in part to changes in industry exploration and development trends, declining mature field production, and active hurricane seasons.

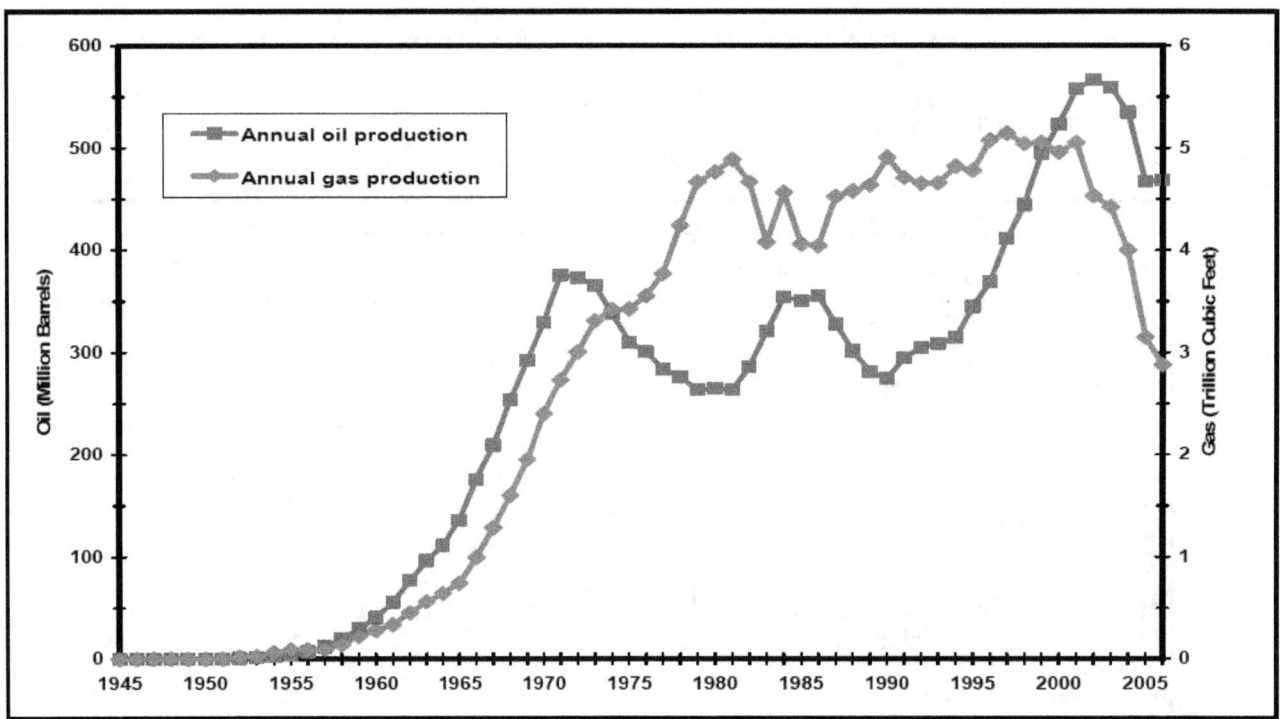

Figure 38. Annual oil and gas production.

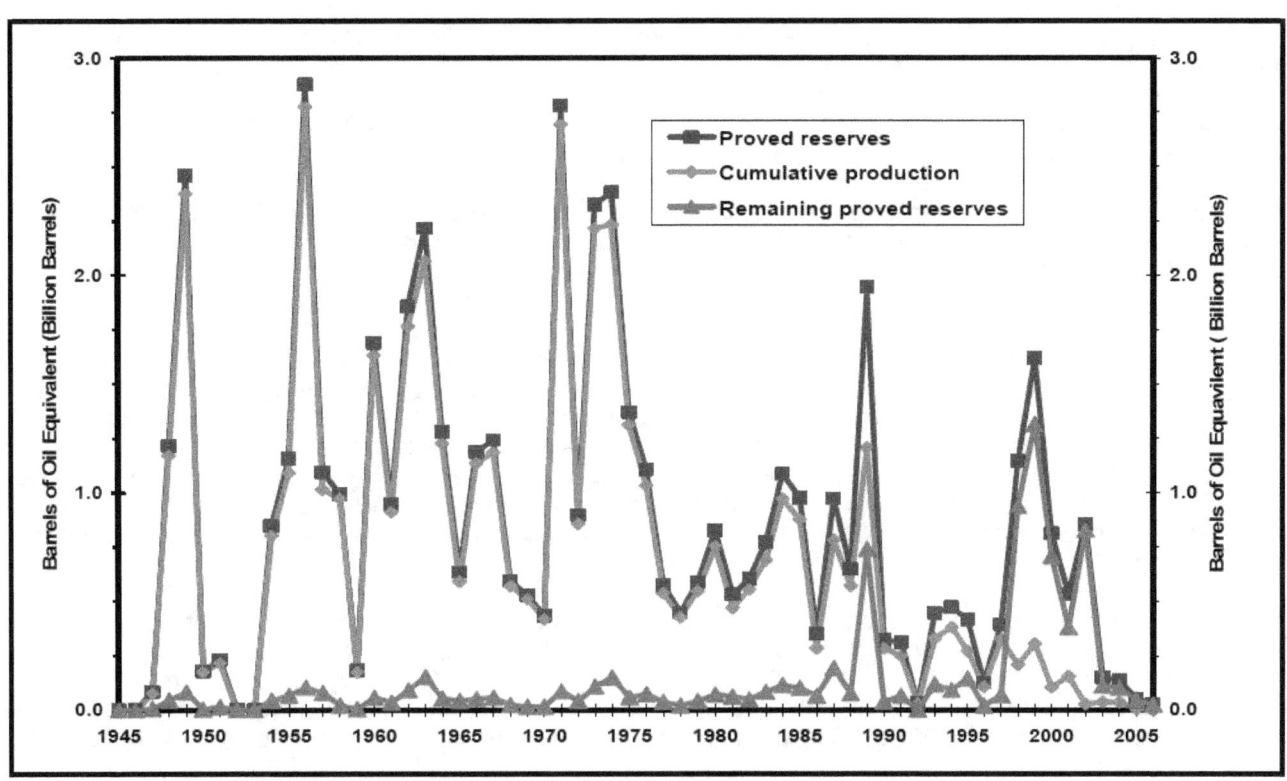

Figure 39. Proved reserves and production by field discovery year.

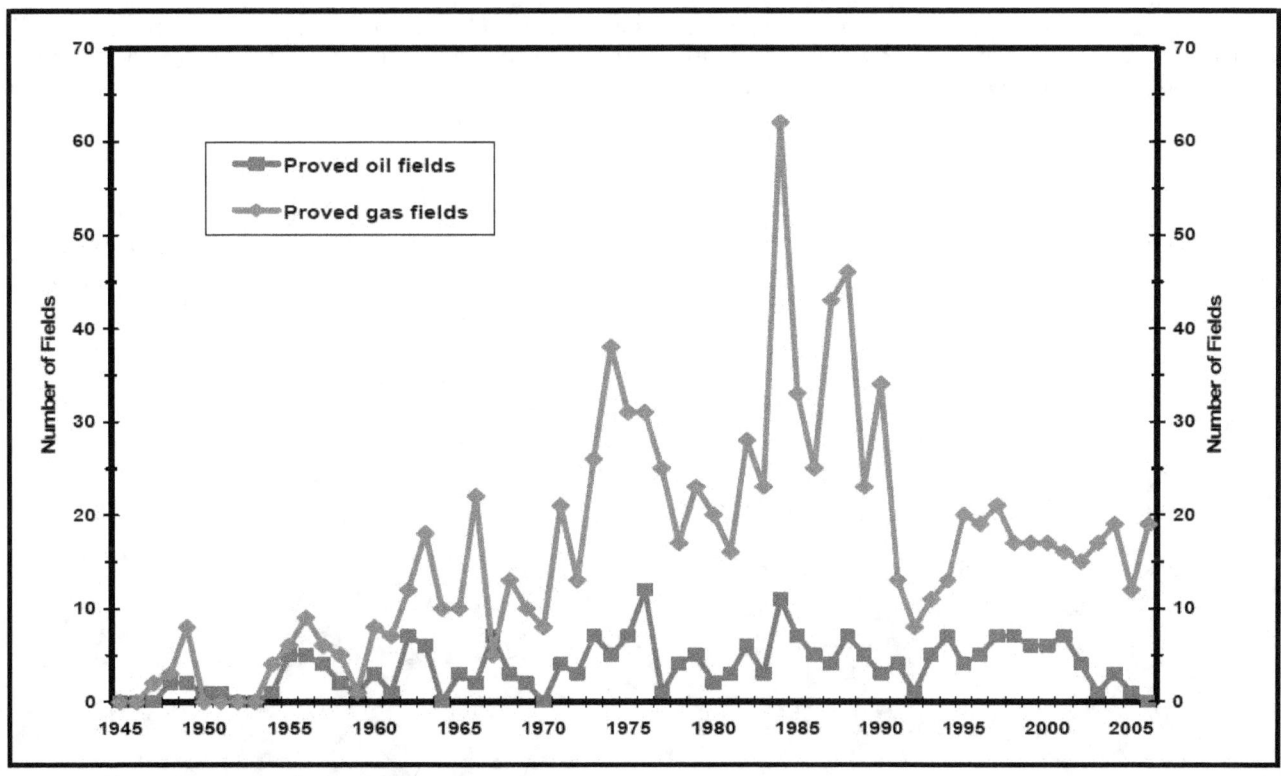

Figure 40. Annual oil and gas field discoveries.

Figure 41 presents the number of proved fields and the mean field size by field discovery year. This plot shows that the number of discovered fields has been decreasing from year to year since 1997, and the mean size of the fields has been getting smaller except for 1989 and 1998 through 2002. Except for the mean field size anomaly in 2005 through 2006 caused by an active hurricane season, the mean field size discovered is expected to increase because of reserves growth and additions in proved fields and reserves from unproved fields that become proved.

Figure 42 presents the number of proved and unproved fields and the average water depth of the fields discovered in each year. For 2001, the mean water depth for the fields discovered peaked at nearly 3,200 ft. Since 1995, the mean water depth has been greater than 1,000 ft, indicating that exploration and resulting production have moved into deeper water.

Figures 43 and **44** show proved oil and gas reserves and annual production by reservoir discovery year. All data presented in **Figure 43** include crude oil and condensate, and all data presented in **Figure 44** include associated and nonassociated gas. The year of discovery assigned to a reservoir is the year in which the first well encountering hydrocarbons penetrated the reservoir. For comparison with the rate of discoveries, the annual production of oil and gas is also shown. In eight of the last ten years, annual proved reserves additions for oil have exceeded annual oil production, resulting in an increase in remaining proved oil reserves. Since 1984, annual gas production has exceeded annual proved reserve additions for gas. In general, annual proved gas reserve additions have declined since the early 1970's.

Figure 45 presents the total footage drilled, the total number of wells drilled, and the number of exploratory and development wells drilled in the Gulf of Mexico OCS each year. All curves show a decline from 1985 to 1986 due to unfavorable oil and gas economics. A second decline occurred from 1990-92. Drilling increased from 1992 to 1997, reflecting stable energy prices and improvements in exploration and production technology. The variation in the number of wells drilled from 1997 to 2006 is caused in part by fluctuation in energy prices and new technologies defining better targets.

Figure 46 presents the number of exploratory wells drilled each year by water depth. The plot shows the move toward drilling in deeper water, but also illustrates continued drilling on the shelf. From 1997 through 2006, the number of exploratory wells drilled in water depths between 201 and 650 ft has reduced by more than 60%. Exploratory wells drilled in water depths greater than 1,300 ft have doubled since 1995. This may in part be due to large discoveries and the availability of more deepwater drilling rigs.

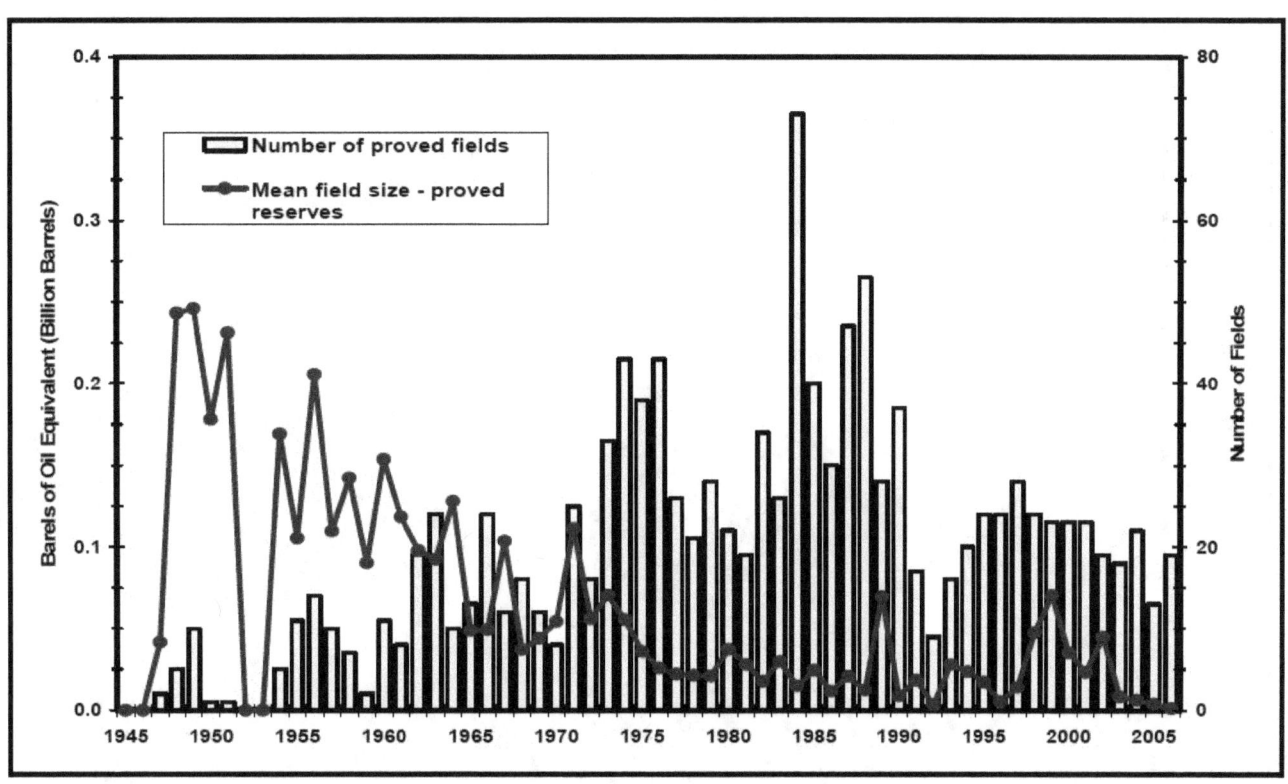

Figure 41. Number of proved fields and mean field size by field discovery year.

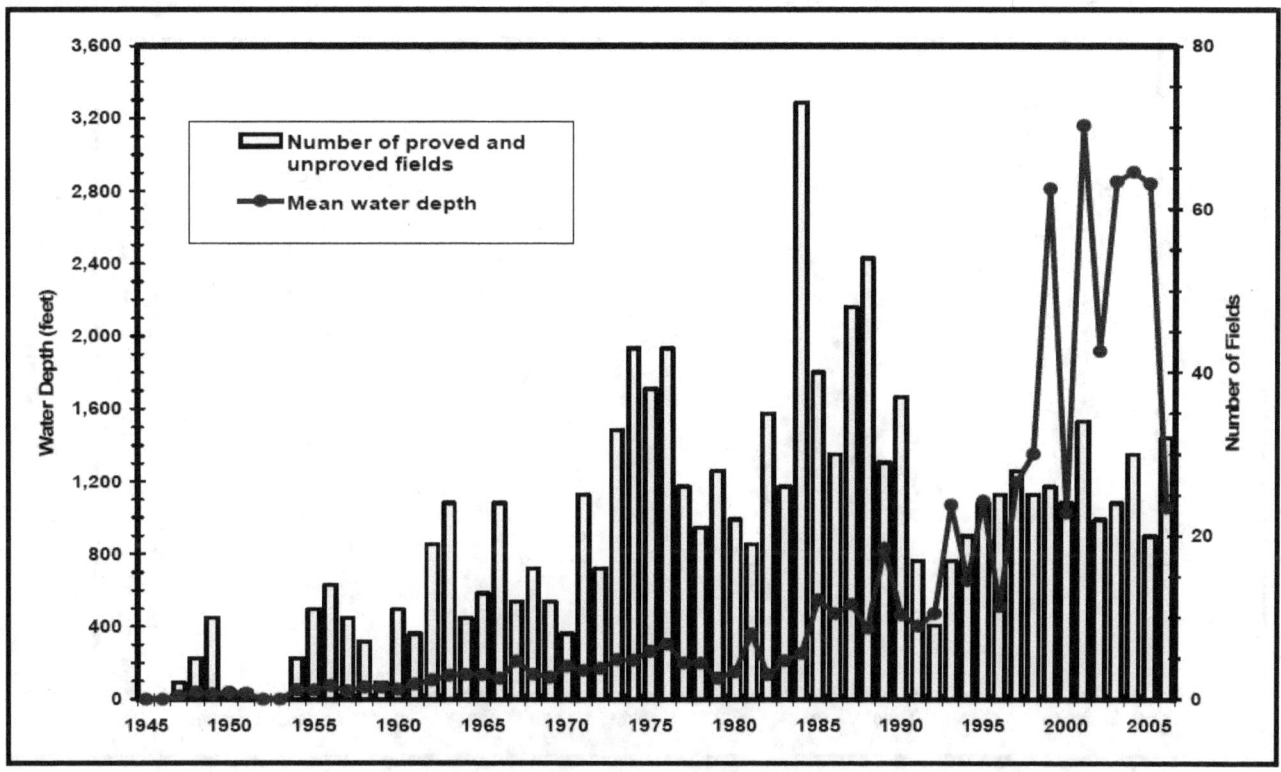

Figure 42. Number of proved and unproved fields and mean water depth by field discovery year.

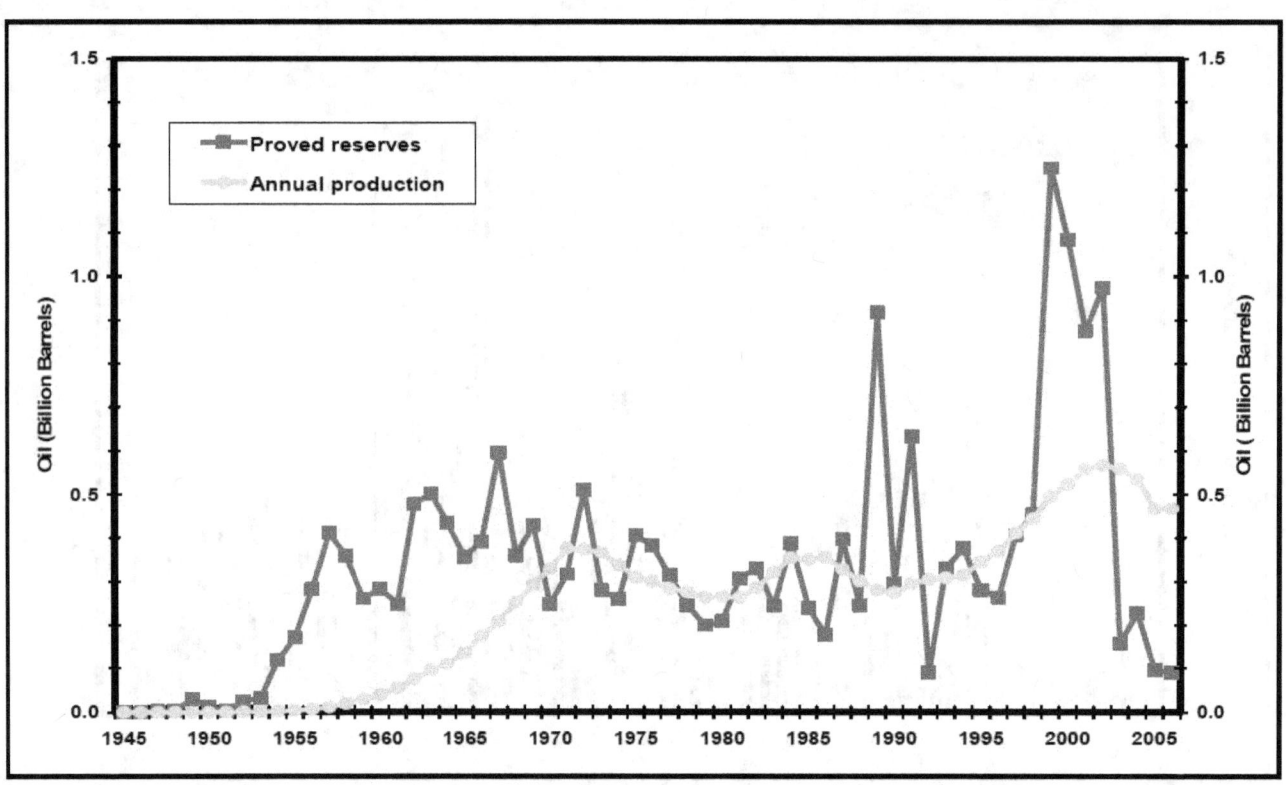

Figure 43. Proved oil reserves by reservoir discovery year and annual oil production.

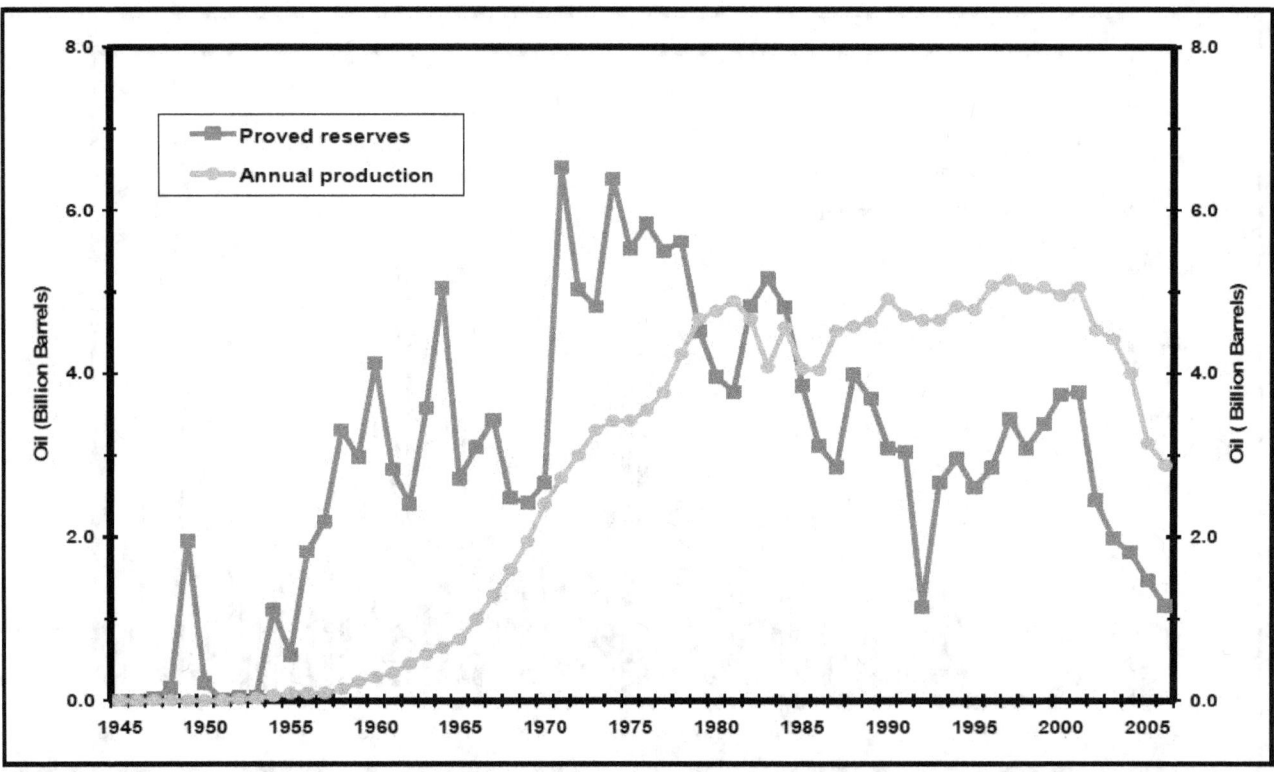

Figure 44. Proved gas reserves by reservoir discovery year and annual gas production.

42

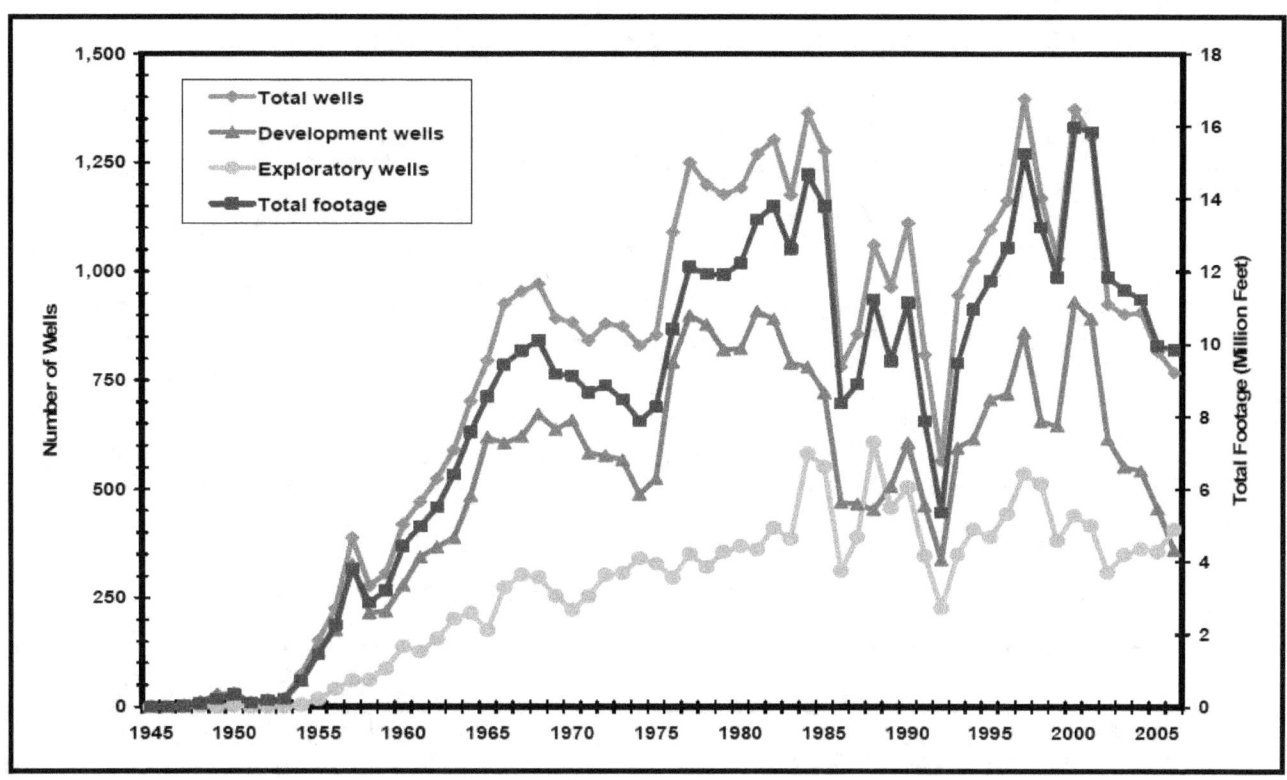

Figure 45. Wells and footage drilled.

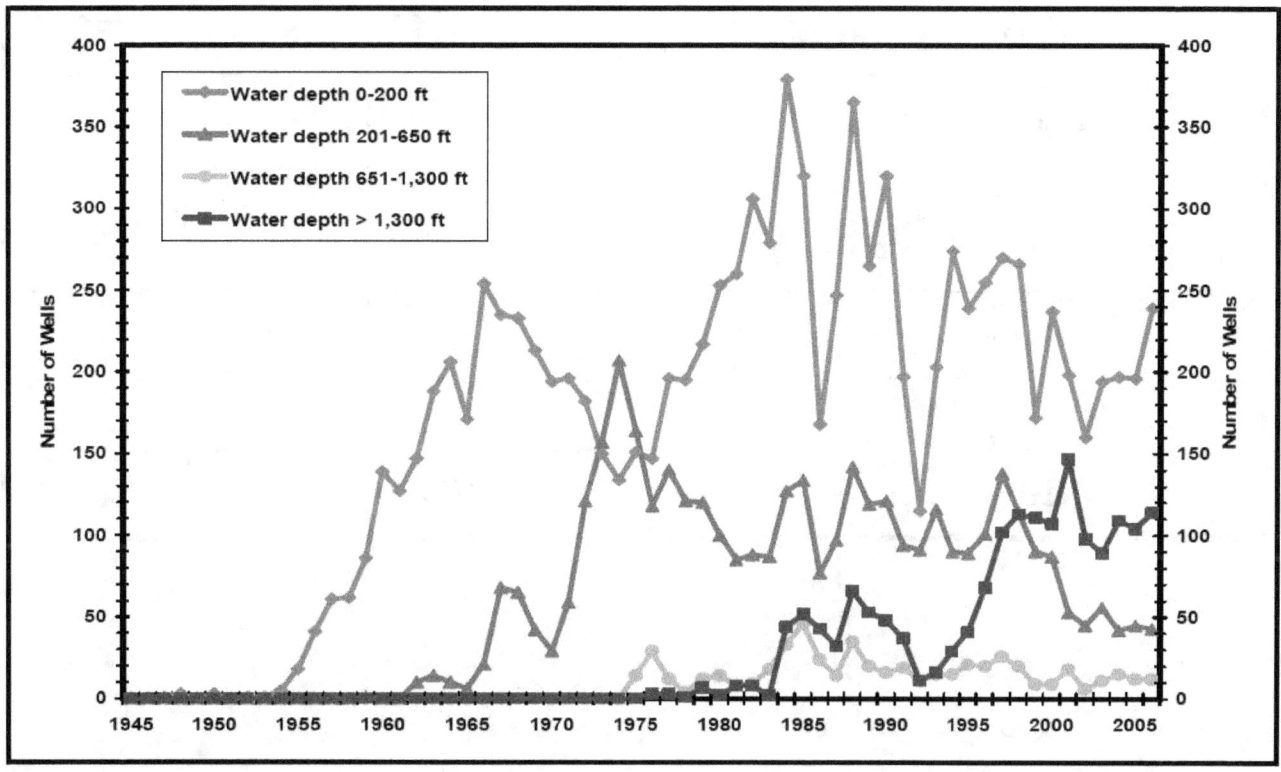

Figure 46. Number of exploratory wells drilled by water depth.

43

Summary and Comparison of Proved Reserves

A summary of the proved reserve estimates for 2006 and a comparison with estimates from the previous year's report (December 31, 2005) are shown in Table 5. There were 34 proved fields added during 2006 (5 oil fields and 29 gas fields), which are summarized and tabulated as increases to proved reserves. Note that 15 of the proved fields added were discovered prior to 2006.

Proved reserve estimates are revised as additional wells are drilled and new leases are added to existing fields, and as reservoirs are depleted and leases relinquished. Complete reevaluations of existing field studies are conducted on the basis of changes in field development and/or production history. Revisions of proved reserves are summarized and presented as changes in Table 5. Based on periodic reviews and revisions of field studies conducted since the 2005 report, the revisions for proved oil and gas reserves have resulted in a net increase. A net change in the proved oil and gas reserves is a result of combining the discoveries and the revisions.

Table 5 demonstrates that the 2006 proved oil discoveries and field revisions exceeded oil production primarily because of lost production as a result of an active hurricane season. The remaining proved reserves increased 6 percent for oil and decreased 6 percent for gas since the 2005 report.

Table 5. Summary and comparison of proved oil and gas reserves as of December 31, 2005, and December 31, 2006.

	Oil (billion bbl)		Gas (trillion cu ft)	
Proved reserves:				
Previous estimates, as of 12/31/2005*	19.8		181.8	
Discoveries		0.29		0.7
Revisions		0.21		1.2
Net Change		0.50		1.9
Estimate, as of 12/31/2006 (this report)		20.30		183.7
Cumulative production:				
Previous estimates, as of 12/31/2005*	14.61		163.9	
Discoveries		0.00		0.0
Revisions		0.47		2.9
Net Change		0.47		2.9
Estimate, as of 12/31/2006 (this report)		15.08		166.8
Remaining proved reserves:				
Previous estimates, as of 12/31/2005*	5.19		17.9	
Discoveries		0.29		0.7
Revisions		0.21		1.2
Production during 2006		-0.47		-2.9
Net Change		0.03		-1.0
Estimate, as of 12/31/2006 (this report)		5.22		16.9

44

Table 6 presents all previous reserve estimates by year. Because of adjustments and corrections to production data submitted by Gulf of Mexico OCS operators, the difference between historical cumulative production for successive years does not always equal the annual production for the latter year. No comparisons will be made for unproved reserves.

Table 6. Proved oil and gas reserves and cumulative production at end of year, 1975-2006, Gulf of Mexico, Outer Continental Shelf and Slope.

Oil expressed in billions of barrels; gas in trillions of cubic feet. "Oil" includes crude oil and condensate; "gas" includes associated and nonassociated gas. Remaining proved reserves estimated as of December 31 each year.

Year	Number of fields included	Proved reserves			Historical cumulative production			Remaining proved reserves		
		Oil	Gas	BOE	Oil	Gas	BOE	Oil	Gas	BOE
1975	255	6.61	59.9	17.27	3.82	27.2	8.66	2.79	32.7	8.61
1976	306	6.86	65.5	18.51	4.12	30.8	9.60	2.74	34.7	8.91
1977	334	7.18	69.2	19.49	4.47	35.0	10.70	2.71	34.2	8.80
1978	385	7.52	76.2	21.08	4.76	39.0	11.70	2.76	37.2	9.38
1979 *	417	7.71	82.2	22.34	4.83	44.2	12.69	2.88	38.0	9.64
1980	435	8.04	88.9	23.86	4.99	48.7	13.66	3.05	40.2	10.20
1981	461	8.17	93.4	24.79	5.27	53.6	14.81	2.90	39.8	9.98
1982	484	8.56	98.1	26.02	5.58	58.3	15.95	2.98	39.8	10.06
1983	521	9.31	106.2	28.21	5.90	62.5	17.02	3.41	43.7	11.19
1984	551	9.91	111.6	29.77	6.24	67.1	18.18	3.67	44.5	11.59
1985	575	10.63	116.7	31.40	6.58	71.1	19.23	4.05	45.6	12.16
1986	645	10.81	121.0	32.34	6.93	75.2	20.31	3.88	45.8	12.03
1987	704	10.76	122.1	32.49	7.26	79.7	21.44	3.50	42.4	11.04
1988 +	678	10.95	126.7	33.49	7.56	84.3	22.56	3.39	42.4	10.93
1989	739	10.87	129.1	33.84	7.84	88.9	23.66	3.03	40.2	10.18
1990	782	10.64	129.9	33.75	8.11	93.8	24.80	2.53	36.1	8.95
1991	819	10.74	130.5	33.96	8.41	98.5	25.94	2.33	32.0	8.02
1992	835	11.08	132.7	34.69	8.71	103.2	27.07	2.37	29.5	7.62
1993	849	11.15	136.8	35.49	9.01	107.7	28.17	2.14	29.1	7.32
1994	876	11.86	141.9	37.11	9.34	112.6	29.38	2.52	29.3	7.73
1995	899	12.01	144.9	37.79	9.68	117.4	30.57	2.33	27.5	7.22
1996	920	12.79	151.9	39.82	10.05	122.5	31.85	2.74	29.4	7.97
1997	957	13.67	158.4	41.86	10.46	127.6	33.17	3.21	30.8	8.69
1998	984	14.27	162.7	43.22	10.91	132.7	34.52	3.36	30.0	8.70
1999	1,003	14.38	161.3	43.08	11.40	137.7	35.90	2.98	23.6	7.18
2000	1,050	14.93	167.3	44.70	11.93	142.7	37.32	3.00	24.6	7.38
2001	1,086	16.51	172.0	47.11	12.48	147.7	38.77	4.03	24.3	8.35
2002	1,112	18.75	176.8	50.21	13.05	152.3	40.15	5.71	24.6	10.09
2003	1,141	18.48	178.2	50.19	13.61	156.7	41.49	4.87	21.5	8.70
2004	1,172	18.96	178.4	50.70	14.14	160.7	42.73	4.82	17.7	7.97
2005	1,196	19.80	181.8	52.15	14.61	163.9	43.77	5.19	17.9	8.38
2006	1,229	20.30	183.6	52.97	15.08	166.7	44.74	5.22	16.9	8.23

* Gas plant liquids dropped from system
+ Basis of reserves changed from demonstrated to SPE proved.

Conclusions

As of December 31, 2006, the 1,229 proved oil and gas fields in the federally regulated part of the Gulf of Mexico OCS contained proved reserves estimated to be 20.30 billion barrels of oil and 183.7 trillion cubic feet of gas. Cumulative production from the proved fields accounts for 15.08 billion barrels of oil and 166.7 trillion cubic feet of gas. Remaining proved reserves are estimated to be 5.22 billion barrels of oil and 16.9 trillion cubic feet of gas for the 956 proved active fields. Remaining proved oil reserves have increased 6 percent and the remaining proved gas reserves have decreased 6 percent from last year's report.

Unproved reserves in the federally regulated part of the Gulf of Mexico OCS are estimated to be 4.44 billion barrels of oil and 8.3 trillion cubic feet of gas. Included are unproved reserves of 4.18 billion barrels of oil and 4.2 trillion cubic feet of gas from 119 fields in water depths greater than 1,000 feet. Estimated unproved reserves for oil are 8.9 times annual oil production, and for gas are 1.4 times greater than annual gas production.

Annual oil production is expected to ramp up as more fields recover from the effects of an active hurricane season, while gas production is expected to level off at rates below those seen in the 1990's. The increase in remaining proved oil reserves is likely to continue as new deepwater discoveries become proved.

In addition to the proved and unproved reserves discussed above, at a minimum there are 1.32 billion barrels of oil and 7.7 trillion cubic feet of gas that are not presented in the tables and figures of this report. This oil and gas occurs on leases that have not yet qualified (and therefore are not placed in a field) or they occur as known resources in proved fields, or as known resources in unproved fields. As further drilling and development occur, these additional hydrocarbon volumes will become reportable, and it is anticipated that future proved and unproved reserves will increase accordingly.

Contributing Personnel

This report includes contributions from the following Gulf of Mexico Region, Office of Resource Evaluation, personnel.

David W. Absher
Kellie K. Lemoine
Lesley D. Nixon
Chee W. Yu

References

Attanasi, E.D., 1998, *Economics and the National Assessment of United States Oil and Gas Resources*, U.S. Geological Survey Circular 1145, United States Government Printing Office, Washington, D.C., Table A-4, p. 29.

Bascle, B.J., L.D. Nixon, and K.M. Ross, 2001, *Atlas of Gulf of Mexico Gas and Oil Sands as of January 1, 1999*, U.S. Department of the Interior, Minerals Management Service, Gulf of Mexico OCS Region, Office of Resource Evaluation, OCS Report MMS 2001-086, New Orleans, 342 p. Internet Web site: http://www.gomr/mms.gov/homepg/gomatlas/atlas.html

Hasseltine, George, 2008, *Indicated Hydrocarbon List, Central, Western, and Eastern Gulf of Mexico*, U. S. Department of the Interior, Minerals Management Service, Gulf of Mexico Region. Internet Web site: http://www.gomr.mms.gov/homepg/offshore/gulfocs/hclist/hclist.html

Crawford, T.G., G.L. Burgess, S.M. Haley, C.J. Kinler, G.D. Klocek, and N.K. Shepard, 2009, *Estimated Oil and Gas Reserves, Gulf of Mexico Outer Continental Shelf, December 31, 2005*, U. S. Department of the Interior, Minerals Management Service, Gulf of Mexico Region, OCS Report MMS 2009-022, New Orleans, 48 p. Internet Web site: http://www.gomr.mms.gov/homepg/offshore/fldresv/resvmenu.html

Nixon, L.D., C.M. Bohannon, M.P. Gravois, E.G. Kazanis, T.M. Montgomery, and N.K. Shepard, 2009, *Deepwater Gulf of Mexico 2009: Interim Report of 2008 Highlights*, U.S. Department of the Interior, Minerals Management Service, Gulf of Mexico Region, OCS Report MMS 2009-016, New Orleans, 72 p. Internet Web site: http://www.gomr.mms.gov/PDFs/2009/2009-016.pdf

Brewton, A., L. Almasy, R. Baud, R. Bongiovanni, T.M. DeCort, A.G. Josey, E.G. Kazanis, T. Riches Jr., M. Uli, F. Yam, *Gulf of Mexico Oil and Gas Production Forecast: 2007-2016*, U.S. Department of the Interior, Minerals Management Service, Gulf of Mexico Region, OCS Report MMS 2009-012, New Orleans, 23 p. Internet Web site: http://www.gomr.mms.gov/PDFs/2009/2009-012.pdf

Lore, G.L., 1994, An Exploration and Discovery Model; An Historic Perspective—Gulf of Mexico Outer Continental Shelf, In: K. Simakov and D. Thurston (eds.), *Proceedings of the 1994 International Conference on Arctic Margins*, Russian Academy of Sciences, Magadan, p. 306-313.

Lore, G.L., D.A. Marin, E.C. Batchelder, W.C. Courtwright, R.P. Desselles, Jr., and R.J. Klazynski, 2001, *2000 Assessment of Conventionally Recoverable Hydrocarbon Resources of the Gulf of Mexico and Atlantic Outer Continental Shelf as of January 1, 1999*, U.S. Department of the Interior, Minerals Management Service, Gulf of Mexico OCS Region, Office of Resource Evaluation, OCS Report MMS 2001-087, New Orleans, 652 p. Internet Web site: http://www.gomr.mms.gov/homepg/offshore/gulfocs/assessment/assessment.html

Lore, G.L. 2006, *Assessment of Undiscovered Technically Recoverable Oil and Gas Resources of the Nation's Outer Continental Shelf, 2006*, U.S. Department of the Interior, Minerals Management Service, Resource Evaluation Division, 6 p. Internet Web site: http://www.mms.gov/revaldiv/PDFs/2006NationalAssessmentBrochure.pdf

Office of the Federal Register, National Archives and Records Administration, 1992, *Code of Federal Regulations, 30 CFR, Mineral Resources*, U.S. Government Printing Office, Washington, D.C.

Society of Petroleum Engineers (SPE), World Petroleum Congress (WPC), American Association of Petroleum Geologists (AAPG), and Society of Petroleum Evaluation Engineers (SPEE), 2007, *Petroleum Resource Management System*, 49p. Internet Web site: http://www.spe.org/spe-app/spe/industry/reserves/prms.htm

U.S. Department of Energy (DOE), 1989, Conversion Factors, *Monthly Energy*, December 1989, p. 132-133.

U.S. Department of the Interior, U.S. Geological Survey and Minerals Management Service, 1989, *Estimates of Undiscovered Conventional Oil and Gas Resources in the United States)–A Part of the Nation's Energy Endowment*, 44 p.

U.S. Department of the Interior, Minerals Management Service, Gulf of Mexico Region, *Gulf of Mexico OCS Deep Gas Update: 2001-2002*, OCS Report MMS 2003-026, New Orleans, 8 p. Internet Web site: http://www.gomr.mms.gov/homepf/offshore/deepgas.html

U.S. Department of the Interior, Minerals Management Service, Gulf of Mexico Region, *OCS Operations Field Directory*, 2007, New Orleans, 178 p. Internet Web site: http://www.gomr.mms.gov/homepg/offshore/fldresv/mastlist.html

Notice

This report, *Estimated Oil and Gas Reserves, Gulf of Mexico, December 31, 2006,* has undergone numerous changes over the last few years. We are continually striving to provide meaningful information to the users of this document. Suggested changes, additions, or deletions to our data or statistical presentations are encouraged so we can publish the most useful report possible. Please contact the Reserves Section Chief at (504) 736-2918 at Minerals Management Service, 1201 Elmwood Park Boulevard, MS 5130, New Orleans, Louisiana 70123-2394, to communicate your ideas for consideration in our next report.

For free publication and digital data, visit the Gulf of Mexico Internet web site. The report can be accessed as an Acrobat .pdf (portable document format) file, which allows you to view, print, navigate, and search the document with the free downloadable Acrobat Reader 9.0. Digital data used to create the tables and figures presented in the document are also accessible as either tab-delimited ASCII text files (.txt; viewable using NotePad or WordPad) or as Excel 97 spreadsheet files (.xls; using Microsoft's Excel spreadsheet viewer, a free file viewer for users without access to Excel). These files are made available in a zipped format, which can be unzipped with the downloadable WinZip program. Soon to be available (for a nominal fee) is a CD-ROM that will include this report, digital data, and field production plots.

For information on purchasing copies of this publication or the CD-ROM contact:

> Minerals Management Service
> Gulf of Mexico OCS Region
> Attn: Public Information Unit (MS 5034)
> 1201 Elmwood Park Boulevard
> New Orleans, Louisiana 70123-2394
> (504) 736-2519 or 1-800-200-GULF
> http://www.gomr.mms.gov

David W. Cooke
Regional Supervisor
Resource Evaluation

The Department of the Interior Mission

As the Nation's principal conservation agency, the Department of the Interior has responsibility for most of our nationally owned public lands and natural resources. This includes fostering sound use of our land and water resources; protecting our fish, wildlife, and biological diversity; preserving the environmental and cultural values of our national parks and historical places; and providing for the enjoyment of life through outdoor recreation. The Department assesses our energy and mineral resources and works to ensure that their development is in the best interests of all our people by encouraging stewardship and citizen participation in their care. The Department also has a major responsibility for American Indian reservation communities and for people who live in island territories under U.S. administration.

The Minerals Management Service Mission

As a bureau of the Department of the Interior, the Minerals Management Service's (MMS) primary responsibilities are to manage the mineral resources located on the Nation's Outer Continental Shelf (OCS), collect revenue from the Federal OCS and onshore Federal and Indian lands, and distribute those revenues.

Moreover, in working to meet its responsibilities, the **Offshore Minerals Management Program** administers the OCS competitive leasing program and oversees the safe and environmentally sound exploration and production of our Nation's offshore natural gas, oil and other mineral resources. The MMS **Minerals Revenue Management** meets its responsibilities by ensuring the efficient, timely and accurate collection and disbursement of revenue from mineral leasing and production due to Indian tribes and allottees, States and the U.S. Treasury.

The MMS strives to fulfill its responsibilities through the general guiding principles of: (1) being responsive to the public's concerns and interests by maintaining a dialogue with all potentially affected parties and (2) carrying out its programs with an emphasis on working to enhance the quality of life for all Americans by lending MMS assistance and expertise to economic development and environmental protection.

MMS *Securing Ocean Energy & Economic Value for America*